An outstanding first book, liv
everyone, on the most impor
rise from the dead, and why
Michael Green

Everyone should read this excellent book. I love its focus on the
most extraordinary event in all history – Jesus rising from the dead
– and the way Dan Clark shows how amazingly relevant it is to the
big questions of life. His writing is fresh, lively and engaging, and
he has a gift for making ideas crystal clear. The real-life stories at
the end of each chapter are great reminders that Jesus' death and
resurrection transforms lives. Enjoy reading *Alive!* and think about
what it's saying, then give it to all your friends.
Tony Watkins

Alive!

What could Jesus' resurrection mean for you?

DAN CLARK

ivp

INTER-VARSITY PRESS
Norton Street, Nottingham NG7 3HR, England
Email: ivp@ivpbooks.com
Website: www.ivpbooks.com

First published in a longer version in 2007 as Dead or Alive?
This edition published 2009

British Library Cataloguing in Publication Data
A catalogue record for this book is available from the British Library.

ISBN: 978–1–84474–408–4

Copyrights

A longer version of the 'Real Lives' interview with Sally Phillips (page 13) first appeared in *Third Way* magazine. Adapted with kind permission.

The 'Real Lives' interview with Abdullah (page 76) is © OMF International. omf@omf.org.uk / www.omf.org.uk. Used with kind permission.

Illustrations © Richard Jones
Typeset in Dante 12/15pt by CRB Associates, Potterhanworth, Lincolnshire
Printed by Ashford Colour Press Ltd, Gosport, Hampshire

Inter-Varsity Press publishes Christian books that are true to the Bible and that communicate the gospel, develop discipleship and strengthen the church for its mission in the world.

Inter-Varsity Press is closely linked with the Universities and Colleges Christian Fellowship, a student movement connecting Christian Unions in universities and colleges throughout Great Britain, and a member movement of the International Fellowship of Evangelical Students. Website: www.uccf.org.uk

Contents

Part 2: Is it true?

Part 3: So what?

Acknowledgments

This is a shortened version of *Dead or Alive?* Particular thanks are due to Julia Evans for helping shorten the book for this edition.

This book is dedicated with gratitude to my parents, who first pointed me to Christ and have always encouraged me in my faith – and who provide a wonderful hideaway for writing.

A brief guide to Bible references used

Matthew 28:1–10 refers to the book of Matthew, chapter 28, verses 1 to 10. Where multiple references come from the same book or chapter, they are separated by a semi-colon or comma. There are various different English translations of the Bible. Most of the time I quote from the New International Version (NIV). On occasion, I have used Today's New International Version (TNIV) or a paraphrase such as *The Message* or the Contemporary English Version (CEV).

Foreword

It's Easter Saturday, and I have just returned with a heavy heart from my local newsagents.

I looked along the paper rack to see if there was any mention of Easter Day. The only acknowledgement of Easter was a tabloid headline: 'Easter Miracle: face of Jesus found on a boiled egg', with the command '"Thou shalt not eat," says Mum'. Apparently a Colorado mother named Linda Bargas is claiming an Easter miracle after some dye she coloured onto a boiled egg dried and transformed itself into the face of Jesus. The message from the news-stand was stark. Easter has nothing to say to the real world of financial crisis, terrorism, family break-up, party conferences and debt. No, actually its only part in the news is to provide weird entertainment for a smirking tabloid audience.

By contrast I have found *Alive!* a fine response. Not least because some of the changed lives it depicts would merit a column in any objective newspaper.

By any standard it is pretty compelling to read about Slobodan, who fought in the Yugoslav army, lost his mother and brother in car and work accidents respectively, and first heard about Christ whilst in a psychiatric hospital. By any standard it is pretty compelling to read of Terry, the first hooligan to be charged with manslaughter after the 1985 Heysel Stadium tragedy, who after his prison sentence and conversion went to Turin, the hometown of Juventus, to seek forgiveness from the bereaved families.

And if these are the headline-grabbing stories in the book, what are the facts behind them? For example, how can Christine, aged forty-five, with inoperable terminal cancer, claim, 'With faith, it's possible to live with it'? How is all this substantiated? I'm delighted to report that Dan Clark gives the honest searcher and indeed the cynical sceptic a great deal of compelling material to consider. Actually there were times when Dan Clark reminded me of Dr Luke, who at the start of his Gospel claims, 'I myself have carefully investigated everything from the beginning' (Luke 1:3).

It all adds up to the fact that I am confronted by the resurrection as an unavoidable issue. Jesus Christ cannot be relegated to the world of the nursery, make-believe and coloured eggs. No. Any rounded debate on suffering, death, religion and meaning has to include this evidence and I loved the way the closing lines of various chapters made that clear:

'If he's now lying in a grave, he can't help us find answers to our questions.'
'We would be left with our questions and our pain.'
'How exactly can Jesus make us alive?'

Rico Tice
Associate Minister, All Souls Church, Langham Place, London

Introduction:
Why should I read a book
about Jesus' resurrection?

I haven't written this book to waste your time. At the moment you might think that whether or not Jesus was raised from the dead is about as relevant as the current weather forecast on Mars. But I've discovered that Jesus' resurrection is the basis of fantastic news for me here and now – news far too good to keep to myself. Millions of others around the world have come to that same realization and have committed themselves to following the risen Jesus. In fact, from the very earliest days of the Christian faith, it's been heralded as 'the *good news* about Jesus and the resurrection'.[1] Wouldn't you like to get some *good* news?

What's more, Jesus' resurrection sheds light on some of the big questions we all ask about life, death, God and meaning. In Part 1 of this book, we'll explore those very questions in the light of Jesus' resurrection. In Part 2 we'll look at the evidence for Jesus' resurrection itself, so that you can come to your own conclusion about whether or not Jesus did come back from beyond the grave, never to die again. Part 3 will unpack exactly why Jesus and his resurrection is such good news for us personally.

But, above all, I don't simply want to persuade you that Jesus' resurrection is relevant and true. Jesus claimed that he came to offer us 'life . . . to the full',[2] so I want to show you that following the risen Jesus is *life-transforming*. Throughout this book, I'll introduce you to a handful of Jesus' followers from around the world, because if Jesus really does offer life to the full, then it must be able to work for anyone and everyone. Meeting these ordinary people is a way for you to judge whether following the risen Jesus actually works.

But why look at *Jesus* and his *resurrection*?

Although he lived 2,000 years ago, Jesus towers over the pages of human history. Great leaders such as Napoleon Bonaparte are still remembered a few hundred years later; I imagine that people like Martin Luther King will be heroes for a few centuries yet. But who else has their birth celebrated as a national holiday in almost 200 countries 2,000 years later?

Today, more than 2 billion people claim to follow Jesus Christ. His birth marks the start of our calendar; his teaching underpins some of our laws; remembrance of his death shapes our school terms. Faith in him has inspired ordinary individuals to great goals: the explorer Sir Francis Drake, the scientist Sir Isaac Newton and the humanitarian worker Mother Teresa – to name but a few – took their lead from Jesus.

If Jesus' life stands far above all others in human history, his resurrection – his bodily coming back to life having been publicly executed – must rank as the single biggest event in world history. No war or natural disaster has had such a widespread, long-term effect. If Jesus had stayed in the grave after his crucifixion on that first Good Friday, the world would have forgotten about him long ago. At best he would feature as a footnote in the history books.

Jesus Christ's resurrection is central to the Christian faith. One of the first Christian leaders wrote, 'If Christ wasn't raised to life, our message is worthless, and so is your faith.'[3] In other words, if Jesus' resurrection is removed, the whole of Christianity collapses into a pile of dust.

So here's my tip: the quickest way to weigh up whether or not Jesus has anything to offer our world is by exploring his resurrection. If the claims about his coming back to life are exaggerated, you can knock Christianity off your list of genuine spiritual options straight away. But if it's true, then it shows us that there is a real spiritual power at work in the world that we can tap into.

Over to you

Many people have never thought seriously about the most influential man who's ever lived. Have *you*? Don't you owe it to yourself to explore the evidence and implications of history's greatest single event – especially because, if it's true, it's good news for you personally?

Real lives - Sally

Sally Phillips is a comedy actress who co-created the Emmy-award-winning Smack the Pony *and featured in the* Bridget Jones *films. More recently, she has appeared in* Skins. *She lives in London.*

Sally, how did you become a Christian, and what difference has it made?

By the time I left university, I was incredibly irreligious. I did a show at the Edinburgh festival called 'Jesus II: He's back from the dead, he's cross, he's everywhere and he wants your soul'. We had a picture of Jesus on the front holding a machine gun. I was very happy with my anti-Christian stance; I felt all Christians wore bad clothes, didn't think things through and were very smug.

Four years later, I started researching a sitcom about witches. Then I started getting very bad nightmares. Working in a very unchristian environment, it was impossible to tell someone about my religious trauma. I'd stand outside bookshops wondering how embarrassing it would be to buy a Bible.

Unusually, I worked with two Christians at a sitcom festival: an actor who was very overt with his faith, and a stand-up who was very private. Six weeks of heated debates later, the actor prayed for me at 3am in Hammersmith shopping centre, and I became a Christian. I felt pretty isolated until the stand-up pointed me to a church where I could make close friends. That church is still home.

Trying to turn my life around was (and remains) hard work. The 'lie amnesty' of '96 was particularly excruciating. Things have definitely changed. Before I became a Christian, my writing was quite unhealthy – full of things I was angry and hurt about. Since I've become a Christian I've done simple characters who are slightly in trouble all the time, but mean well. That's how I experience my Christian walk.

At the beginning I had people shouting at me because they were frightened that I'd judge them, and frightened that it's true. Recently I've really sensed a change – perhaps because I'm more confident in my own faith and denying Jesus less!

Part 1

Is it relevant?

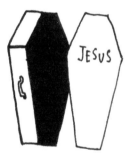 

How can Jesus' resurrection help us find answers to life's big questions?

1. Is there anybody out there?

At some point in our lives, we begin to ask big questions. When we are waiting for yet another bus, or putting in the umpteenth load of washing that week, we wonder whether there's more to this life than dull routine. When a friend's life is turned upside down by accident or illness, we ask why there's so much suffering in the world. When a relative dies, we think about what will happen when we die.

These are the sorts of question we'll be looking at in these first chapters:

- Questions about purpose: what is the point of life?
- Questions about destiny: what happens when we die?
- Questions about suffering: why is there so much in our world?
- Questions about 'God': does he/she/it exist? If so, what is he/she/it like?

These questions often give us a headache if we consider them for too long, so we just get on with life without discovering any answers. Or the bus suddenly turns up, and we forget that the question even began to form in our mind. Life does not always make much sense, and that not only hurts us, it disappoints us as well. Deep down, we would love to find some answers.

My conviction is that Jesus – and in particular, his resurrection – is a key that helps to unlock some answers to life's big questions. At first sight, it's an unlikely-looking key – 2,000 years old, and made in a place and culture far removed from our own. Yet the questions we ask are the same ones that people have been asking since the beginning of time.

You may not believe that Jesus lived, died or really did come back from the dead – in other words, that the key even exists! (We'll come back to that in Part 2.) But for the time being, I'd like to invite you to imagine: 'Just *suppose* that Jesus' resurrection *is* true . . . ' Let's see if the key fits . . .

Searching for the Other

Have you ever had your breath taken away by nature's beauty? I can vividly remember driving through a mountain range, struggling to keep my eyes on the road because I desperately wanted to soak up the majesty of the views around! At moments like these, words aren't enough. Our spirits somehow seem to be lifted onto a higher plane.

Some parents describe holding their newborn child as 'a miracle' or 'a spiritual moment'. Even those who call themselves agnostics – who are not sure whether or not there is a god – would agree that it is experiences like these that make them think twice about the supernatural.

Opinion polls in the UK report that about 70% of the population believe in a god of some sort or another, but there is increasing uncertainty about what such a god is like. Comedian and writer Spike Milligan was once asked if he ever prayed. 'Yes,' he said, 'I pray desperately, all the time: get me out of this mess. But I've no idea who I'm praying to.'

Despite this uncertainty, interest in 'spirituality' is growing fast. People are seeking inner peace. Many are looking to alternative or Eastern views of the gods for inspiration. Some look to 'Mother Earth'. Others look to 'the god in me'. But even these spiritualities provide little certainty.

Many of us *think* there is someone out there, and at heart most of us *hope* that there is, but, if we are honest, our best guesses are still stabs in the dark. Our question remains: Is there anybody out there? If so, what is he/she/it like? Indeed, how can we find out?

Is there anybody out there?
If so, what is he/she/it like?

What if God was one of us?

Suppose a girl from rural Africa visits England. She's heard about the Queen, but she has no idea what the Queen's like – blonde hair, thirties, long legs? She goes to Buckingham Palace, and is so excited to be at the Queen's home that she jumps up and down and waves her arms, shouting out to the Queen, trying to encourage her to come out, but she's told the Queen isn't there. The girl is devastated. In fact, she becomes convinced that the Queen doesn't even exist at all. She goes to feed the ducks in the park instead.

Of course, what that girl really needed was for the Queen to come out onto her balcony and wave at her – or better still, to stroll outside onto the Mall and chat with her – even to go and feed the ducks with her.

Sometimes, we can be like that child, trying to guess what 'God' is like. But at the end of the day, what we really need is for 'God' to make itself known. If it doesn't do that, it's easy to conclude that 'God' doesn't exist.

The Christian claim is that, despite living in heaven, God *has* come down into the real world, walking and talking with real humans. God has chosen to make himself known in a way that we can understand. The hit song 'What if God was one of us?' asked,

> If God had a name, what would it be?
>
> . . .
>
> If God had a face, what would it look like?'

If we'd been alive in Israel 2,000 years ago, we could have seen God face to face in the person of Jesus – and we could have found out what he's like. It's a huge claim, but what is it about Jesus' life, teaching and resurrection that can prove it?

Jesus' life and teaching give evidence of a supernatural power

Anyone who reads one of the four earliest surviving biographies of Jesus (known as the 'Gospels') will know that Jesus was an extraordinary man, and virtually everyone agrees that he had access to a supernatural power, which was shown in many ways. For example:

Jesus' teaching. Jesus' moral, ethical and spiritual teaching left the crowds 'amazed . . . because he taught them as one who had authority', unlike the religious experts of his day.[1] All the great spiritual leaders since Jesus, and even some non-religious leaders, have applauded his teaching, and encouraged others to follow it.

Jesus' power to heal. Doctors today can heal many diseases with expensive medical treatments. By contrast, Jesus healed people with just a touch of the hand or a word of command. The Gospels even record occasions when people who had died were brought back to life at his command. Not surprisingly, 'At this, onlookers were completely astonished.'[2]

Jesus' power over nature. Weather experts can sometimes forecast when storms are going to occur, but they cannot stop them happening. In a boat being tossed about on a stormy sea, Jesus told the storm to calm down, and it did! His fellow travellers were terrified and asked each other, 'Who is this? Even the wind and waves obey him!'[3]

Today, people question such accounts (we'll look at whether they're historically reliable in Part 2), but, at the time, no-one doubted that this impressive list of miracles actually happened: even those who opposed him admitted as much.[4] They were the first to agree that Jesus had access to a supernatural, divine power.

However, it is clear that Jesus thought himself to be more than just a man with *access* to a divine power; his words and actions often implied that he himself *is* that God. The religious 'experts' of the day (who didn't like Jesus' ministry) were among the first to realize this: on one occasion, they muttered, 'He must think he is God!'[5] They could see that his extraordinary actions and powerful teaching backed up his claims to be God.

Jesus' resurrection prompted people to worship him as God

If Jesus' life gives a strong indication that there is someone out there, and that he claimed to be God, it is his resurrection that confirms his claim. No mere human can overcome death. But if there *is* a God who created life, then that God could overcome death as well. And if Jesus is God, we shouldn't be surprised that he rose from the grave.

It's useful to look at people's reactions to Jesus after his resurrection. The two women who were the first to see him 'came to him, clasped his feet and worshipped him'.[6] Another of Jesus' close friends, Thomas, had a similar reaction. At first doubtful about Jesus' resurrection, once he'd touched Jesus physically, he stopped doubting. His words were simple but profound – calling Jesus, 'My Lord and my God!'[7]

It's important to realize that these were men and women who, although they firmly believed in God, did not expect God to turn up in front of their eyes, and wouldn't have dreamed of worshipping a fellow human. In fact, their whole belief system had to be completely turned upside down to make room for this idea that Jesus was God. This background makes the first Christians' claim that Jesus was God even more remarkable.

Initially convinced that Jesus was an evil man, one man changed his mind having seen the resurrected Jesus for himself, and wrote that Jesus was 'declared with power to be the Son of God, by his resurrection from the dead'. Elsewhere, he described Jesus as 'the image of the invisible God'.[8]

A few months ago, our house was burgled. The police came and checked for fingerprints but they couldn't find any. You could say that the police were looking for the image of the (now) invisible burglars, but failed.

When Paul described Jesus as 'the image of the invisible God', it's as if he's saying, 'We've got a match! We know exactly what God looks like now, because we've got his fingerprints as evidence!'

The guessing games are over

This means that the days for guessing are over. It would be impossible to speak with certainty about what God is like – unless you have concrete evidence. The combination of Jesus' extraordinary life and claims, backed up by his unique resurrection from the dead, never to die again, point us to the conclusion that he is God in human flesh. We don't need to guess any more about *whether* God exists, because he has shown himself in Jesus. We don't need to guess any more about what God is *like*, because in Jesus we can see exactly what he's like.

- On reading about Jesus' dealings with the sick and bereaved in his day, we discover that God is extremely caring: on many occasions, Jesus was 'deeply moved', 'filled with compassion', or wept alongside hurting people.[9]

- We find that God is interested in people no matter what their background or history. Jesus mixed with an extraordinary variety of people (prostitutes, farmers, tax-collectors and political leaders; partygoers and social recluses), and crossed social, political, religious and racial boundaries. Jesus often spotted individuals in a crowd and met them at their point of need.
- Jesus was particularly radical in his attitude towards women: in a society that viewed them as second-class, Jesus was not embarrassed to spend time with women and count them among his followers.[10]

In all this, it's clear from the vast crowds that followed Jesus wherever he went that he appealed to ordinary people. In fact, Jesus was very clear that his target audience wasn't the religious; it was those who weren't interested in organized religion.

Is there anybody out there?

If the Christian claim that Jesus rose from the dead is true, then our searching for 'somebody out there' can stop, because we will have concrete evidence that there is a God. More than that, Jesus' teaching and life show us clearly what God's character is like – and he's wonderful, compassionate, loving and good. Jesus taught that God created us, loves us, and wants each of us to know him personally, as our 'Father'.

However, if Jesus did *not* rise from the dead, we are no better off in our search for the something or someone who makes sense of those spiritual moments. Those who knew Jesus may have marvelled in his presence, but if he's now lying in a grave, he can't help us find answers to our questions.

Real lives – Addlan

Addlan comes from China and is doing a science doctorate at the University of Manchester.

Addlan, how do you know that God exists?

Growing up, I thought that matter and material things were all that existed: I didn't believe in any gods. I believed that things had positive and negative sides, and harmony could be achieved only by mixing them properly. However, I felt that my life was lacking something so I started to learn ancient and modern philosophy and even tried to practise Buddhist meditation in order to understand the world around me. My mind was confused and my heart troubled. I needed peace desperately.

After arriving in the UK, I went to a café run by Christians to help international students settle down here, where I made some Christian friends. At first, I didn't believe that someone's life could change simply by accepting Jesus as their Saviour. However, I found that Christians were nicer, more peaceful, and very friendly.

As a scientist, I am struck by the beauty of the universe, and think that it must be designed, not random. I learned from my new friends that the Bible says human beings were created by God in his own image, and that God has wisdom and God is love. The facts that there are laws and orders governing this universe and that love exists in human beings make me believe that there is a God.

Once I realized that God exists and God loves me, I studied the Bible more and decided to follow Jesus. I know that I have changed a lot. Before I was a Christian, I was envious, untrusting, judgmental, selfish, complicated and hopeless. But those attitudes were very destructive, hurtful and painful. I worried, I felt desperate, I was lonely and my heart had no rest. However, since I became a Christian, I have become simpler, and I feel released and healed.

2. Why hasn't God done something about all the suffering?

We're so used to seeing the destruction caused by earthquakes, tsunamis, floods, hurricanes, famines and other disasters on television that we're in danger of becoming immune to the plight of countless millions of our neighbours in this world. Almost every day another suicide bombing is reported, and world leaders are trying to work out how best to conquer international terrorism.

But even if our lives aren't affected by disaster and terrorism, they are seldom free from pain. Whenever our dreams are shattered, or we find our nightmares turning real, we bury our head in our hands and cry out 'Why?' Empty answers from well-meaning friends only serve to make things worse.

Of course, if there is *no* God, then we cannot blame him for life's tragedies. We can only guess that suffering is a natural part of life, with little hope of its ending. But when Christians claim that there *is* a God, the problem of suffering becomes all the more pointed: not just 'Why has this happened to me?' but 'Why has *God* let this happen to me?'

After all, Christians say that God is both loving and all-powerful. If God is all-powerful, he should be able to do something to stop the suffering. If God is loving, he cannot *want* people to suffer. Therefore, if suffering happens, it is either because God is not all-powerful or because he is not loving. Even in the Bible, people shout at God,

> Wake up! Do something, Lord!
>   Why are you sleeping? . . .
> Why do you keep looking away?
>   Don't forget our sufferings
>   and all our troubles.[1]

In a brief chapter like this, I cannot hope to answer all these questions. I simply want to show how Jesus' life, death and resurrection provide a key that begins to unlock new perspectives on the problems of suffering.

Jesus suffered and can therefore comfort us

Jesus' public execution was by no means his first experience of suffering. One man predicted that Jesus would be 'a man of sorrows, and familiar with suffering',[2] and this description was painfully accurate. His parents hadn't been married for nine months when Jesus was born (a shocking thing in those days); he was a refugee; he was ridiculed by his family; he was homeless for a while; his closest friends abandoned him; he was lonely; he lived under an oppressive regime that reviled him; he mourned the loss of close friends; he was tried on false charges before a biased court and was tortured and then sentenced to one of the cruellest forms of death ever invented. If Jesus is God, then it is true to say that God himself has suffered and died. He knows what our pain-filled lives are like, and he hurts with us. God isn't lounging around in some heavenly deckchair, unconcerned about human suffering. Jesus has experienced more suffering than many of us ever will.

God isn't lounging around in some heavenly deckchair

But why does God go to such lengths to suffer? One of the first Christian pastors explained that Jesus 'had to enter every detail of human life', so that 'when he came before God . . . he would have already experienced it all himself – all the pain, all the testing – and would be able to help where help was needed'.[3] One of the early Christian leaders testified to the reality of this comfort. He endured beatings, prison, riots and shipwrecks, yet described God as 'the Father of compassion and the God of all comfort, who comforts us in all our troubles'.[4] Jesus suffered so that he can bring us comfort in our sufferings.

That's all very well. But does Jesus offer anything more than just a 'crutch for the weak'? What I've said so far still begs the question, 'Why hasn't God done something about all the suffering?'

Jesus' death and resurrection was a battle against evil

Suppose you go to see your doctor with chest pain, worried that something could be wrong with your heart. The doctor listens through his stethoscope, smiles, and then launches into a long and complicated diagnosis of the problem. Feeling even more anxious, you interrupt, blurting out, 'But can you do anything about it?'

Intellectual explanations about suffering are not always much help. We need a solution to our pain. When Jesus died on the cross, God was beginning to deal with the very existence of evil and suffering, and our main enemy, death.

The Bible pictures Jesus' death as the turning point in the war between God and evil. Evil's worst weapon is death (which is why so many people are scared of death); so if Jesus were to conquer evil, he had to disarm death itself. The only way Jesus could disarm death was to meet it head on, personally. That is what happened when he was executed: Jesus 'shared in [our] humanity so that by his death he might destroy him who holds the power of death'.[5]

As Jesus died, it seemed as though death had won. Yet the battle was not over. Jesus' resurrection is the evidence that Jesus fought *and won* the battle against evil on the cross. 'It was impossible for death to keep its hold on him'[6] is how one person put it. If, having died innocently, Jesus was then raised from the dead, he has shown us that death, our ultimate enemy, is not unbeatable.

If we are on Jesus' side, we are on the winning side, for 'he suffered death, so that by the grace of God he might taste death for everyone'.[7] Rather than death defeating us, God 'gives us the victory through our Lord Jesus Christ'.[8]

Jesus' resurrection ushers in the new creation

But if Jesus has defeated death, why do people still die?

In any war, there is often a key battle after which the eventual outcome of the war is certain, but, sadly, the fighting continues. Unwilling to admit defeat, the loser carries on trying to inflict damage on the side that has already won. It takes a while before the inevitable outcome is confirmed.

The Bible pictures the war between God and evil as a cosmic war, on a cosmic timescale, which unfortunately means that, although the key battle was won 2,000 years ago in Jesus' death and resurrection, the war is still going on. The eventual outcome is certain – evil and death will be banished; peace will reign for ever. We just don't know when that will happen. Jesus' resurrection, then, doesn't just remind us to look for a glimmer of light in our darkest moments; it dazzles us with the glorious and certain hope that a day will come when all suffering will stop, and that we can be part of that blissful reality. How does that work?

The Bible says that God created the world as a perfect place, and that one day he will recreate that perfection in the 'new creation'. This new creation will have more in common with *this* world than with the Hollywood caricature of heaven's long-bearded inhabitants sitting on fluffy clouds! Jesus let one of his friends see the new creation in a dream:

> I saw a new heaven and a new earth, for the first heaven and the first earth had passed away . . . And I heard a loud voice from the throne saying, ' . . . [God] will wipe every tear from their eyes. There will be no more death or mourning or crying or pain, for the old order of things has passed away.'

He who was seated on the throne said, 'I am making everything new!'[9]

In the new order, all suffering will vanish. Imagine a world with no doctors, because everyone will be healthy; a place with no need for lawyers, because there'll be no arguments; a world without international tension or war, so no police or soldiers or peace-keeping forces. Imagine a world with no wheelchairs or Zimmer frames; no need for mouth braces, acne cream or pacemakers.

In the Bible, Jesus' resurrection acts as the guarantee that this wonderful new creation will become a reality.

Some questions remain

I will never have all the answers to suffering, and I do not pretend that what I've written answers all your questions, or even mine. But Jesus' life, death and resurrection show us that God himself experienced human suffering. They also reassure us that he *has* done something about suffering, he *is* doing something about it, and he *will* do something about it.

These Christian perspectives on suffering are quite unique, and give reassurance for the present and hope for the future. Evil will not have the last laugh. But, of course, if Jesus did *not* die and rise again, then such reassurance and hope are without foundation. We would be left with our questions and our pain.

Real lives – Slobodan

Slobodan fought in the Yugoslav army in the 1990s, and after meeting with Jesus Christ, studied at a Bible school in Serbia.

Slobodan, how can you believe in God when you've suffered so much?

I was a high-school dropout, and when I started working most of my money was spent on alcohol and cigarettes. After National Service, I got involved in gambling as well.

In 1991, civil war broke out. One night, at 3am, the military police came to call me up. We were given uniforms and ammunition and were sent to a town in Croatia that was under a fierce attack. I saw my friends around me dying and losing body parts. That was the first time I started thinking about God. I said to him, 'If you exist, get me out of this hell in one piece.'

I came back in one piece, but not in good health. My life continued to go downhill. My mother was killed in a car accident; my father threw me out of the house; my brother was killed in a work accident. I became a squatter, lonely and completely unable to cope with my pain. I became very aggressive. My friends began to avoid me.

In 1999, NATO invaded our country and I cried out to God again. I tried committing suicide and was placed in a psychiatric hospital. I met a guy who was visited by young people who talked to him about Jesus. I met with them too and when I was discharged I attended my first church service. I felt warm inside and tears ran down my face. I prayed and became a Christian.

I've realized that I can't live in my own strength. When I go through difficult situations now, God helps me view them in a very different way. I don't get depressed or reach for false comforts any more. If Jesus had not given his life for me, I would still be living in ignorance, agony and darkness.

3. What happens when we die?

I once took part in a project that asked people their opinions on this subject. The answers were varied. Some responded that they thought they would cease to exist: this life is all there is. Many responded that they believed in a heaven, but not a hell. Others were equally sure that there was both a heaven and a hell. One thing was sure: of those who believed in a hell, very few imagined they would go there! The majority of us believe that, as long as we try our best, and our good deeds outweigh our bad deeds, we will go to heaven/paradise/a better place. People are surprised to learn that this idea that heaven is a *reward* for a good life is more like the Muslim understanding of the afterlife than the Christian one.

Thoughts about what happens when we die are often at best guesses or simply wishful thinking. None of us can be sure what happens unless someone comes back from the dead to tell us. If Jesus did rise from the dead, he is precisely the person to tell us. His resurrected body gives us clues as to *what* our bodies will be like after we die, and he is the one who can speak with authority about *where* we'll be.

None of us can be sure what happens unless someone comes back from the dead to tell us

Jesus' resurrection shows us *what* we'll be like after we die

As we read the accounts of Jesus' post-resurrection life, we find that he had a recognizable physical body, which was partly similar to his pre-death body, and partly different. He could talk and eat as he did before, but he could also 'appear' and 'disappear', apparently at will. He still had the scars from his crucifixion, but they didn't seem to affect him. We'll examine these accounts in more detail in Part 2.

The important thing for now is to pick up from Jesus the clues about what our own bodies will be like after we die. The clue is that we, too, will be resurrected. The Bible says that 'in Christ [a title for Jesus] all will be made alive'.[1] Jesus' resurrection is a guarantee that *all* people will have a new life after death.

This means that, after we die, we will not cease to exist, nor will we be reincarnated as different beings, nor will we be spirits floating on clouds! Rather, we will have similar physical bodies to the ones we have at the moment, but without our existing illnesses and imperfections.

If that gives us a strong clue about *what* our bodies will be like after death, what does Jesus say about *where* we will be?

Jesus warned us about hell

In Christmas carols, we sing that Jesus is 'gentle, meek and mild'. But writings about Jesus record him saying some very harsh words, and giving uncomfortable teaching, not least on the subject of heaven and hell.

Jesus spoke frequently of hell as a real place, where some people would be sent. When talking about what would happen at the end of time, he said, 'This is how it will be at the end of the age. The angels will come and separate the wicked from the righteous and throw them into the fiery furnace, where there will be weeping and gnashing of teeth.'[2]

Some people joke about wanting to go to hell because 'at least my friends will be there'. But there will be no friends in hell. In fact, Jesus tells us it will be a place where all God's good gifts from this life are absent.

Imagine a place without trust, friendship, peace and beauty. Jesus hints that hell will be like that. I would not wish anyone – even my worst enemy – to land up there.

Some people believe in purgatory as a temporary alternative to hell, from where everyone graduates to heaven having 'done their time' for any evil deeds committed in this life. As an idea, it's very appealing, especially after reading Jesus' teaching about hell! However, Jesus never mentioned purgatory, but he did give every indication that hell is real.

Jesus told us about the wonderful reality of heaven

Fortunately, the answer to our question ('What happens when we die?'), according to our 'been there, done that' tour guide, Jesus, is not all doom and gloom. Jesus also spoke wonderfully of the 'kingdom of heaven'. 'The kingdom of heaven is like treasure hidden in a field,' he said. 'When a man found it, he hid it again, and then in his joy went and sold all he had and bought that field.'[3] Finding the kingdom of heaven is like finding a priceless treasure.

What will heaven be like? The Bible tells us,

> What God has planned
>   for people who love him
> is more than eyes have seen
>   or ears have heard.
> It has never even
>   entered our minds!'[4]

It will be beyond our wildest imagination.

Some people imagine heaven to be intensely boring, floating in the air, but the picture the Bible paints is one of wonderful community: 'After this, I saw a large crowd with more people than could be counted. They were from every race, tribe, nation, and language.'[5] Heaven will also be a place of perfection, where 'there will be no more death, suffering, crying, or pain. These things of the past are gone for ever'.[6]

Most importantly, heaven is described as a place of deep friendship – with each other, and with God. For the Christian, the crowning glory of heaven is that 'God's home is now with his people. He will live with them, and they will be his own . . . He will wipe all tears from their eyes'.[7] To wipe someone's tears from their eyes is a beautifully intimate act, and describes the closeness of the relationship that the Christian has with God.

As a Christian, I look forward to heaven as I might excitedly look forward to seeing an old friend, knowing that I'll have all the time in the world to spend enjoying their company. Heaven will be all that we long for this life to be. I can't wait to get there!

Which is it to be: heaven or hell?

Crucially, Jesus said that the difference between those who go
to heaven and those who end up in hell was not how good or
religious we are in this life, or how hard we try, but how we
respond to Jesus and his claims.[8] We will look more closely at
that in Part 3. For now, the points to absorb are these: if Jesus
did rise from the dead,

- Jesus' own resurrected body shows us that we will have
  similar bodies to our current ones after we die, yet
  without aches, pains and defects;
- Jesus speaks with authority about where we will go when
  we die. As the one person who has come back from the
  dead, he is the only one who can tell us for definite what will
  happen when we die. He speaks of hell and heaven as being
  real: hell worse than awful; heaven better than glorious.

This is all very well, but slightly other-worldly! For many people,
the question of what happens when we die isn't an intellectual
one; it's a personal one they're forced to face by the news that
they have a terminal illness. Can Jesus' resurrection say anything
to them?

Jesus' resurrection gives Christians hope in the face of death

Film-maker Woody Allen joked, 'It's not that I'm afraid to die;
I just don't want to be there when it happens.' He's not alone
– many people are afraid of dying and death. But if Jesus rose
from the dead, then death is not the end, and we can have hope
in the face of death.

When one of Jesus' closest friends, Lazarus, had died and been in a tomb for four days, Jesus said to Lazarus' sister Martha, 'I am the resurrection and the life. Anyone who believes in me will live, even though they die; and whoever lives by believing in me will never die.'[9] To prove his claim, Jesus proceeded to bring Lazarus back to life. Later on, Lazarus was to die again, unlike Jesus. But Jesus had made his point: he has power over death, so those who trust in him need not fear death.

My grandfather once went to two funerals on the same day. One was a humanist funeral, and he described it as empty of hope. Death was the end, and the person leading the funeral could say nothing of comfort in the face of death. If Jesus has not risen from the dead, we have no grounds for hope as we approach death.

The other funeral was that of a Christian, and my grandfather described it as an almost joyful event. Certainly, there was sadness, but there was also gladness, because the dead man had gone to be with his Saviour and Friend, Jesus Christ. If Jesus did rise from the dead, we can have hope in the face of death.

Real lives – Christine

Christine is forty-five, married with five daughters and two grandsons. Her own parents both died by the time she was thirteen. Eight months before writing this she was diagnosed with cancer and given six months to live.

Christine, how does being a Christian make a difference to you as you face death?

By my late twenties, I had three daughters and two divorces. Wanting my children to meet some stable families, I started going to my local church. People were very friendly and generous. It wasn't hard to go each week.

The minister prompted me to make a decision that he said would change my life. I didn't have anything to lose, so I did. No flashing lights, nothing remarkable at all. But everything began to change. I stopped drinking and flushed my antidepressants away without suffering any physical reactions. I lost my totally irrational fear of dying at night. I was a million miles from the victim I'd let myself become.

My terminal cancer diagnosis came out of the blue. I didn't realize how much Jesus had made a difference until I heard a man get the same diagnosis as me. He was desperate. His family were silent apart from platitudes. What else could they say?

The diagnosis didn't hit me like that. Oh, it hurt like nothing else. I don't want to leave my family, my husband, my life. I've already passed my 'sell-by date'. In Asda I'd be worth less now, but through the care and prayers of Christians, I feel more valued than I've ever felt. Cancer isn't the worst thing that's ever happened to me. With faith, it's possible to live with it.

Before the diagnosis I had hoped that the future in heaven was better than here. Now, inside, I have a certainty. I can't explain that, but my knowledge is built on experience and academic study. The first accounts in the Bible say witnesses 'saw' Jesus after he'd died. He proved it to lots of doubters. I know it holds true from past experience. I just wish I could persuade more people to believe!

4. Does life have a meaning or purpose?

A Buddhist professor said, 'The chances that life just occurred on earth are about as unlikely as a typhoon blowing through a junkyard and constructing a Boeing 747.' That leaves each of us with a nagging question in our minds. As Madonna put it, 'I'm sure everyone's had that out-of-body experience where you say to yourself . . . why am I here?'[1]

Some people try to find a meaning in life by being good to those around them, or providing a better world for their children.

But many lack meaning and purpose. Prince Charles has said, 'There remains deep in the soul, if I may use that word, a persistent and unconscious anxiety that something is missing; some ingredient that makes life worth living.'[2] One columnist observed that many live

. . . lives of quiet, and at times noisy, desperation, understanding nothing but the fact that there is a hole inside them and that however much food and drink they pour into it, however many motor cars and television sets they stuff it with, however many well-balanced children and loyal friends they parade around the edges of it . . . it aches.'[3]

Many try to ignore this ache by keeping themselves busy. Even Bob Geldof, who has given so much time and effort to help those living in poverty in Africa, admitted, 'I am unfulfilled as a human being.'[4]

Others use drink or drugs, partly to escape the boredom of life.

But is it true that there is no meaning or purpose in life? Or could Jesus' life, death and resurrection provide clear direction to our meandering path through life?

Jesus' resurrection tells us that life's meaning is found in the light of eternity

Jesus made the incredible claim, 'I have come that [those who follow me] may have life, and have it to the full.'[5] Far from draining all the juice from life, being a follower of Jesus is the way to finding true meaning in life. How?

Many of us look to money and material things to provide meaning and happiness, even though lots of rich and famous people tell us that money has not made them happy.

Kenneth Williams, the hugely successful British actor, wrote in his diary, 'I wonder if anyone will ever know the emptiness of my life?' Jesus repeatedly warned his listeners against finding meaning in the material things of this life. 'Watch out!' he said. 'Be on your guard against all kinds of greed; life does not consist in an abundance of possessions.'[6]

Instead, he says that true satisfaction comes through understanding our lives from an eternal perspective. Jesus' resurrection shows us that there *is* life beyond the grave, and that there is a spiritual side to our lives. There is an alternative to living for the moment, and that is to live for eternity by storing up 'a treasure in heaven', which, unlike material wealth, is guaranteed, because it can't wear out or get stolen.[7] There is an alternative to our frequently selfish lives: living for God. Jesus promised that to those who 'seek first [God's] kingdom and his righteousness . . . all these [material] things will be given to you as well'.[8]

Jesus' resurrection tells us that we can find meaning through a friendship with God

There is a saying in psychology that a person does not know *who* they are until they know *whose* they are. In other words, our closest relationships help to provide our identity. Our human experience is that relationships can give the highest joy in life, so it's natural that many find purpose and meaning through their closest relationships. But where a relationship is broken or missing, we also experience the deepest heartache. Freddie Mercury, one of the greatest pop stars ever, blamed his loneliness on his success:

> You can have everything in the world and still be the loneliest man, and that is the most bitter type of loneliness. Success has

brought me world idolisation and millions of pounds, but it's prevented me from having the one thing we all need – a loving, ongoing relationship.'[9]

His loneliness is repeated in millions of hearts around the world. We long for a 'loving, ongoing relationship', but such relationships are so hard to find.

It is not surprising that the second part of Jesus' answer to our search for meaning and purpose in life is to point us to a relationship that is 'loving and ongoing'. Such a friendship is possible with God, the one who made us, through Jesus, the one who died yet is alive again.

A Christian is someone who *knows* God – not just by knowing facts about him, but knowing him as friend. In the Bible, Abraham was described as God's 'friend'.[10] Jesus' own definition of 'eternal life' was that people 'may *know* . . . the only true God, and Jesus Christ, whom [God] has sent'.[11] Jesus taught his followers to call God their 'Father', showing that they could have a very close relationship with God.[12] Years after Jesus' death and resurrection, the early Christian leader Paul said, 'Nothing is as wonderful as *knowing* Christ Jesus my Lord.'[13] So when Christians pray, they are not talking to thin air; they are talking to the living Jesus who can hear and answer their prayers.

Jesus' own definition of 'eternal life' was that people 'may know God'

Those who know God confirm that his love is constant. God describes himself as 'the compassionate and gracious God, slow to anger, abounding in love and faithfulness, maintaining love to thousands, and forgiving wickedness'.[14] That is a stunning and beautifully tender claim, which many of God's friends in the Bible and many Christians since can back up. God's love is also unconditional: even when Christians let God down, he still sticks by them.

Jesus' coming back to life, never to die again, means that he is alive today, and that we can know him, even though we cannot see him. Jesus says that our deepest longings are satisfied through knowing the God who made us.

Our human hearts were made by God, for God, and our inner emptiness will end only when we begin a friendship with God. Maybe our emptiness is like a 'homing instinct'. Swallows and other birds confidently fly to countries thousands of miles away. Although we often do not realize it, we have something like a 'homing instinct' that is trying to take us back to our Maker.[15] For some people, that process takes years. Many, tragically, ignore their homing instincts, and never find their way 'home'.

Augustine was a thinker who searched for years to find meaning and purpose. After he became a Christian, he prayed to God, 'You have made us for yourself, and our heart is restless until it rests in you.'[16]

Does life have a meaning or purpose?

Jesus said that he came to give life in all its fullness, and the experience of millions of Christians is that he does just that. His resurrection alerts us to the fact that our meaning comes through the perspective of eternity. Jesus said, 'I am the bread of life. Whoever comes to me will never go hungry, and whoever believes in me will never be thirsty.'[17]

Of course, if Jesus did not rise from the dead, we are thrown back into the bleak reality of searching desperately for meaning in life where there is none; still hunting for that perfect relationship that can't be found.

Real lives – Slava

Slava is a waiter in Russia, studying to become a film director.

Slava, what difference has being a Christian made to you?

Before I met Jesus, I was filled with cynicism, and an all-consuming desire to get noticed. I made lots of jokes, usually to prove others ridiculous and myself smart. I had been passionate about all kinds of achievement, hoping to find happiness in that. I desperately wanted people to depend on me and love me, so I strived to earn money, to become the best in mathematics, to buy beer for friends . . . But all this didn't work, and pain and loneliness wouldn't leave me . . .

I came to know Christ through meeting a man at my local church who could loan me money. I hated worship songs and despised all the Christians, but soon I heard about Jesus and his death, which could prevent me going to hell. I had no choice but to come to Christ and offer him my life. I thank God that he loved me so much and knew me so well that he found a way to my heart.

Knowing Christ has made all the difference. In him I've found a love I couldn't dream of. But I also realized that I was no different from others: the bad things they would do to me, I would do myself. But Christ has made me different. Since I felt his love, he's been teaching me how to love others. I've learned to respect people and to appreciate what they have inside more than outside. I've discovered the freedom to be myself, and to make mistakes. And relationships matter a whole lot now because I know I don't have to be afraid of them. They're risks worth taking. My life with Christ is worth living.

5. Which religion, if any, is true?

Within a couple of miles of my home, I can walk to several Muslim mosques, a Sikh temple, a Baha'i information centre, a variety of different Christian churches and a Jewish synagogue. If I wander into a bookshop, the 'religion and spirituality' section includes books on spiritual ideas that I have never even heard of. To someone with no experience of religion, the choice is overwhelming. How could any religion possibly make an exclusive claim to be 'true' when there are so many alternatives?

It is very common for someone who doesn't know much about religion to suppose that all religions lead to God and that no single religion can claim to be superior to any other. It is an attractive idea. However, it has two basic problems.

- To say 'All religions lead to God' is a claim to a superior knowledge about God and religions – it is doing precisely what it tells others to avoid!

○ Ordinary believers in some of today's world religions realize that their different understandings of 'God' are incompatible. For example, a Buddhist's claim that the ultimate reality is a Void, an Emptiness, cannot match up with a Jew's claim that God is a personal being. A Muslim's claim that there is only one God doesn't fit with the Shinto believer's claim that there are many gods.

Several of the major world religions state that they are the *only* way to understand God correctly, and that other religions are wrong. They're either all wrong, or one may be true. For example, Islam cannot be right in saying that Judaism is wrong if Judaism is also right in saying that Islam is wrong.

How, then, can we be sure which religion's claims, if any, are true? Can Jesus' life, death and resurrection speak clearly through the noise of different answers? I want to suggest that Jesus is unique among the founders of world religions, and that the Christian accounts of his death and resurrection are far more reliable, historically speaking, than other accounts. If these points are true, Jesus' claim to be the only way to God should be the starting point of any serious spiritual enquiry.

Is Jesus unique among the founders of world religions?

Jesus' life and death are unique among religious leaders

Moses died, according to Jewish tradition, at the age of 120. He was the hero of the Jewish nation.

Buddha died at the age of eighty. He was surrounded by a great host of devotees, whom he had won to his way of thinking.

Confucius died at the age of seventy-two, having returned home in triumph and successfully organized a large company of followers to continue his work.

Muhammad was ruler of a united Arabia when he died aged sixty-two, in the arms of his favourite wife.

Some people claim that the origin of all religions is basically the same: that they are the creation of men of great personal devotion who uncover some basic human truths and devote their lives to teaching those truths, perhaps forming a culture or subculture around them. As far as Judaism or Buddhism or Confucianism or Islam go, there is truth in that opinion.

Christianity's founder has a strikingly different story. Jesus died somewhere around the age of thirty-three, after a teaching ministry of at the very most three years. He had been betrayed and denied by his own supporters. He had been mocked by his opponents. He had been abandoned by everyone, even, he said as he was dying, by God himself. He suffered one of the most brutal and humiliating forms of death ever devised. His followers scattered, and the future of his movement appeared doomed.

Yet while members of some other world religions *commemorate* the death of their founder, Christians actually *celebrate* Jesus' death regularly. The contrast between Jesus and the founders of other world religions could hardly be greater.

At least two of the major religions are wrong about Jesus

In Part 2 of this book, we will examine closely the historical *evidence* surrounding Jesus' death and resurrection. This section will simply look at the differing *claims* that Judaism, Islam and Christianity make about those events.

52 | ALIVE!

As the Jewish scriptures date from before Jesus, they have no record of his life, but the traditional Jewish understanding is that Jesus died on the cross, and remained dead. To them, his death was deserved and proves that he wasn't the Messiah. Having initially emerged from Judaism, Christianity had soon been forced out over the crucial issue of Jesus' death and resurrection, as the Jewish authorities tried to stop the Christians from spreading their message.

The Islamic scriptures (the Qur'an) were written hundreds of years after Jesus. He is mentioned several times, and is even called the Messiah. Muslims honour Jesus as a prophet, and, like Christians, believe that Jesus was born of the virgin Mary and will come back one day. However, when it comes to the events surrounding Jesus' death, the differences begin. Speaking of Jesus' death, the Qur'an says, 'They did not kill him and they did not crucify him, but it appeared so to them . . . they did not kill him for certain.' Rather than being killed, 'Allah took him [Jesus] up to Himself' (Surah 4:157–158). Some Muslims believe that it was not Jesus upon the cross, but someone else who looked like Jesus. Other Muslims believe that it *was* Jesus on the cross, but that he did not die; it merely looked as if he died, whereas in fact Allah had 'taken him directly to himself'.

In contrast to Jews and Muslims, Christians believe that it was Jesus who died on the cross, and that he did come back to life, never again to die.

These three differing versions of the events of that first Easter cannot all be true. It's vital that we get to the truth on this crucial historical question – but how?

In any historical investigation, the most reliable information is that written closest to the events under examination. So when it comes to examining the competing claims about Jesus' death and resurrection, which are the earliest – and therefore most reliable

– documents? The Qur'an was written by one man, nearly 600 years after Jesus' death and resurrection, and there is no other written supporting evidence for its claims. By contrast, most of the Bible's varied accounts of Jesus' death and resurrection were written forty to fifty years after the initial events, some much earlier. There is further evidence within seventy years of the events.[1]

Not surprisingly, no academic historian gives the Qur'anic accounts much weight in comparison to the accounts written over 500 years earlier – and very close in time to the original events being described.

Jesus' resurrection and its implications are unique

Muhammad's body is buried at Medina. Nobody claims that he rose from the dead. The Buddha's body was cremated. Nobody claims that he rose from the dead. Moses was buried in Moab. Nobody claims that he rose from the dead.

Christianity is unique in claiming that its historical founder rose from the dead. Nobody could produce the body as proof that he was still dead, even though it was supposedly under Roman guard after his crucifixion.

It did not take long for Jesus' followers to realize that his resurrection had huge implications. An early Christian statement of faith said that Jesus 'was declared with power to be the Son of God, by his resurrection from the dead'.[2] Among other things, it was Jesus' resurrection that made them claim he was actually God – a claim just as controversial then as it is now.

Which religion, if any, is true?

Jesus stands out as unique among the great religious leaders the world has seen. If Jesus did not rise from the dead, he is not unique, and he can be relegated to one idea among many. But if he did rise from the dead, we must take his claim to be God with the utmost seriousness. Furthermore, when trying to work out which (if any) of the religions are true, it makes sense to start by weighing up the Christian claim that he rose from the dead. As one writer put it:

> If Jesus did rise from the dead, then he is indeed the way to God. God has vindicated him and set him on high. In that case the exclusiveness of the Christian claim makes sense. It does not amalgamate with other faiths, because it is so very different. The risen Jesus is not just one of the many, he is unique. It is not that Christians are narrow-minded or uncharitable about other faiths. But if Jesus is indeed, as the resurrection asserts, God himself who has come to our rescue, then to reject him, or even to neglect him, is sheer folly. That is why Jesus is not, never has been, and never can be, just one among the religious leaders of mankind. He is not even the best. He is the only . . . If we conclude that Jesus Christ did indeed rise from the dead, then that settles the question of other religions.[3]

Let the investigation begin!

Throughout Part 1, we've found that the life, death and resurrection of Jesus form a key that begins to unlock some answers to life's big questions. That makes it all the more important to determine what actually happened that first Easter. If the Christian claims about Jesus are true, we have met God himself in the person of Jesus, and we have started to find answers to life's biggest questions. If the Christian claims are shown to be false, the answers that I've given in these chapters are also false. It's time for our detailed investigation to begin.

Real lives – Abdullah

Abdullah, a Malay, lives in a rural Muslim village in South-East Asia. He is now getting on in years, but used to work as a rubber tapper. He is married and has six children.

Abdullah, what made you leave Islam and follow Jesus?

My friend Yusuf was a convicted criminal and spent ten years of his life behind bars. But on his release from prison he was a different man. His life had completely changed. He was friendly and polite. His relationship with his wife improved. He became a helpful and cheerful person.

One day, I asked him what had caused such a change. He replied by asking me, 'Where is Isa al-Masih at present?' (Isa al-Masih is the Muslim title for Jesus Christ. Muslims believe that Isa – Jesus – was a prophet of God, and that he is presently alive with God in heaven, having been rescued from earth before crucifixion.)

I answered, 'Isa is in heaven with God!'

Yusuf asked me a second question, 'And where is Muhammad, the prophet of Islam, at present?'

'The prophet lies dead in his grave,' I answered.

Yusuf smiled and then he asked me, 'So, Abdullah! Whom do you want to follow? A dead prophet or a living one?'

I was speechless. I stood there with my mouth open, but could not say a word. I had never thought about this matter before (I was happy as I was), but somehow I knew that this was the most important question of my life.

Yusuf's words would not leave me alone. Muhammad is dead. Jesus Christ is alive. If Jesus lives and is coming back again, then he must be almighty. If he is really alive, then I must put my faith in him. I could do nothing else but follow him.

I wanted to find out more, so I saw Yusuf again the next day and together we visited some Christian friends of his. They explained many things about Jesus to me. Then we prayed together and I committed my life to Isa al-Masih – Jesus Christ.

Names have been changed to protect identities. Yusuf was later killed, for being a Christian.

Part 2

Is it true?

Investigating the evidence about
Jesus' resurrection

6. Looking at the evidence

Seventeen men were recently arrested in Crete and charged with offensive behaviour – because they were dressed as nuns, flashing their thongs. But at their trial, no-one turned up to testify against them. Without witness evidence, their case collapsed, and they were released.

It's time now to look at the *evidence* for Jesus' resurrection. If there isn't any evidence for it, my case collapses. The answers that began to open up in Part 1 to the big questions we all ask would turn out to be useless.

So in Part 2, I'm no longer asking you to *suppose* that Jesus rose from the dead; I'm asking you to *investigate* the evidence carefully. This chapter will present the evidence as we've received it down the centuries.

It's time to put your thinking caps on . . .

1. Evidence from non-Christian sources

Besides all the records in the Bible, there are several ancient historians who describe Jesus' life, and many other early religious writings that speak about Jesus. There is so much evidence for the existence of a man called Jesus that no serious historian doubts he existed. But what was his life like? We'll start by looking at the accounts found outside the Bible, written by those who weren't Christians.

The most famous Jewish first-century historian was called Josephus. He wrote:

> About this time arose Jesus, a wise man, if indeed one ought to call him a man. For he was one who wrought surprising feats and was a teacher of such people who accept the truth gladly.[1]

Josephus talks about Jesus' miracles and teaching. Associating Jesus with wisdom and truth, he even acknowledges that he was no normal human. But what about Jesus' death?

Again, very few historians doubt that Jesus really did die, because ancient historians who were around at the time mention his execution. Tacitus, the greatest of Roman historians of the period, confirms that Jesus Christ

> suffered the extreme penalty during the reign of Tiberius at the hands of one of our procurators, Pontius Pilatus, [in] Judea.[2]

The crunch question is whether or not Jesus came back to life

The crunch question is whether or not Jesus came back to life. Josephus describes how after the crucifixion those who had in the first place come to love him did not give up their affection for him. On the third day he appeared to them restored to life, for the prophets of God had prophesied these and countless other marvellous things about him. And the tribe of Christians, so called after him, has still to this day not disappeared.[3]

Although this passage is slightly disputed by ancient historians, it is clear that, at the least, Josephus knew that Christians claimed that Jesus had come back to life three days after he died.

Tacitus also implies that the Christian sect had gained a new lease of life sometime after Jesus had been executed, relating how the movement spread to Rome.

These two non-Christian sources (along with others[4]) provide broad support for the claims that are made in the Bible: that Jesus lived, died and rose again. But for more details of the events of the first Easter weekend, we must turn to the Gospel accounts.

2. Evidence from Christian sources[5]

Thursday night: the arrest and trials
On Thursday evening, Jesus shared his last meal with his twelve disciples, in Jerusalem. It was the traditional Jewish Passover meal, but rather than the usual celebration, there was a sense of foreboding. Jesus talked of his coming death, and predicted that one of those sharing the meal would betray him. They then walked out of the city to a nearby garden. Jesus prayed in great distress whilst his disciples fell asleep. Late that night, Jesus was arrested by armed servants from the Jewish religious authorities, backed up by a detachment of Roman soldiers (they had been tipped off by Judas, one of Jesus' disciples).

The Jewish religious authorities were keen to get rid of Jesus, because he was challenging their authority, and making illegal claims. However, they had no power to pass the death penalty, so once they had found Jesus guilty, they then had to persuade the Romans that he was also a political threat to them, and therefore worthy of being killed. Because of this Jesus faced several different trials during the night.

He was taken to Caiaphas, the high priest, who asked Jesus, 'Are you the Christ, the Son of the Blessed One?' Jesus replied, 'I am.' The Sanhedrin (the group of religious leaders who acted as judges) agreed this was a claim to be God, a crime worthy of death.

Friday: the day of execution

The Sanhedrin sent Jesus to the Roman governor, Pontius Pilate, to face charges for being a political threat to the Romans. Pilate wasn't sure what to do. The crowds were pressurizing him and eventually he condemned Jesus to death.

Jesus was severely beaten and ridiculed by the soldiers, with a mock crown, made of thorns, jammed on his head. Once at the execution site, Jesus would have had his out-stretched arms nailed to a wooden cross-beam at the wrist, his legs pushed up to one side and his feet nailed to an upright beam. Eventually, he would have died of suffocation, unable to pull himself up sufficiently to breathe. Despite the extreme pain that Jesus suffered as he was being crucified, he prayed for his executioners, 'Father, forgive them.'

After about six hours, Jesus died. To confirm his death, a soldier pierced Jesus' side with a spear.

A wealthy follower of Jesus, Joseph of Arimathea, asked permission to place his body in an unused tomb carved out of rock. The mourners did not have time to wash and anoint Jesus' corpse for proper burial before nightfall, as Jewish custom decreed, so as a temporary measure the body was wrapped in linen and packed with a large amount of dry spices. A heavy stone was placed over the tomb's entrance.

Saturday: the day of rest

As the rest of the city continued to celebrate the festival of Passover together, Jesus' friends and family were in shock as they tried to come to terms with his death. After sunset on the Saturday some of the women went to buy spices ready for the Sunday morning, when they planned to wash and anoint Jesus' body properly.

Meanwhile, the religious leaders wanted to guard the tomb from attack by his devoted followers. So a group of guards was placed outside the tomb.

Sunday: the day of surprises[6]

The women got a surprise when they arrived at the tomb. The heavy stone that had been covering the entrance had been rolled away. As they entered the tomb they saw an angel, who announced to them, 'Jesus, who was crucified . . . is not here; he has risen, just as he said.' The angel then told the women to 'see the place [within the tomb] where he lay,' after which they ran away. Soon afterwards, Peter and John also confirmed that the body was gone, leaving the linen burial cloths behind.

Mary Magdalene was the first to meet the risen Jesus, although in her grief she first thought he was the gardener before recognizing him. Shortly afterwards, the group of women who had seen the angel at the empty tomb met Jesus. On both occasions, Jesus told the women to tell the other disciples the good news.

Peter seems to have been next to meet the risen Jesus, although the location is not recorded. Then on the Sunday afternoon,

Jesus joined two dejected disciples on the road out of Jerusalem to a nearby village, although they too did not recognize him at first. When they did, Jesus disappeared from their sight, and they ran back to Jerusalem to announce their news to the larger group. As they did so, Jesus appeared in the room, showed the disciples his scars and ate some food with them.

The next forty days: further appearances

No more appearances by the risen Jesus are recorded until the following Sunday, when he appeared again to the disciples. This time Thomas was with them. He was highly sceptical of the other disciples' excited stories, saying, 'Unless I see the nail marks in his hands and put my finger where the nails were, and put my hand into his side, I will not believe it.' When Jesus appeared, he invited Thomas to do exactly that, and Thomas believed.

In total, twelve separate appearances of the risen Jesus are recorded in the Bible.

It is important to note that no records state that Jesus died a second time. The disciples firmly believed that Jesus' resurrection body was a transformed one. For example, he was sometimes difficult to recognize at first, but he clearly still had scars from the crucifixion. Similarly, he apparently appeared and disappeared at will, yet he could still be touched and perform normal actions such as eating. The main difference was that Jesus' body was no longer able to die. The disciples clearly believed that Jesus was still alive as he ascended into heaven, forty days after the Easter weekend.

This chapter has recounted the bare bones of the Christian claim: that Jesus died and rose again. But should these records be classified as fact or fiction? And what of Jesus' bones: is he dead or alive?

7. Is the evidence reliable?

A few months ago, an animal rights activist was accused of fire-bombing Oxford University. Part of his defence was that DNA evidence linking him to an exploded device was unreliable. Every jury must decide whether or not the evidence and witnesses presented to them are reliable. If the witnesses are lying, they should be ignored. So it is with Jesus' resurrection. The last chapter presented the eyewitness evidence. This chapter asks whether it is reliable. So, here are some brief answers to the most common questions people ask about the Gospels.

Weren't the four Gospels written many years after the events?

Scholars debate exactly when the four Gospels were finished, but it is most likely that they were written between thirty and sixty years after Jesus' death and resurrection.[1] That sort of timescale is a relatively safe one for a document to be considered reliable, because if the Gospel accounts were inaccurate, the documents would have been hotly disputed at the time by witnesses.

The individual stories and sayings in the Gospels were widely known long before they were written down:

- The stories would have been passed on accurately by word of mouth. (Many of the first Christian leaders were Jews who were well practised at accurately memorizing large portions of religious material.)[2]
- Scholars are agreed that the stories would then have been collected, written down and widely circulated.[3]
- Only after that would the Gospels themselves have been written as well-crafted, finished products.

Thus, the material in the finished Gospels was not 'new'; the writers merely collected, refined and carefully structured the already well-known stories for a wider audience. The fact that their Gospels were published between thirty and sixty years after the events they described does not automatically make them unreliable; their accuracy should be judged on the quality of their research and the reliability of their sources. Let's look briefly at the individual Gospels.

Mark's Gospel
Mark's Gospel was probably the first to be finished. Mark used Peter (a close friend of Jesus) as his main source.

Matthew's Gospel
Matthew's Gospel was probably written by one of Jesus' twelve disciples, so it is largely an eyewitness account. He also

supplemented his own evidence with other written sources, particularly writing to suit a Jewish audience.

John's Gospel

John's Gospel was also probably written by another of Jesus' closest friends, providing further eyewitness details. Some of the material isn't found in the other Gospels, but it would be wrong to conclude that it's made up. It's likely that John had seen the other Gospels and knew he didn't need to repeat what had already been said. It would be rather like trying to publish a new biography of Sir Winston Churchill today, when so many already exist. To be a success, the new book would need to include 'exclusive new material'.

Luke's Gospel

Luke tells us how he got the information for his Gospel in his introduction. He tells us that he did not see the events himself, but that he 'carefully investigated everything from the beginning' and that he aimed to write 'an orderly account', so that his readers 'may know the certainty' of what they had previously heard. His accounts are based on recollections that 'were handed down to us by those who from the first were eye-witnesses'.[4] Luke is a model historian.

Is there any other evidence to support the Gospel materials?

In the last chapter, I described how the non-Christian ancient writers Tacitus and Josephus both directly mention Jesus' life and death and refer to the Christian claim of his resurrection.

Several other ancient writers refer to Christians and their practices, but Josephus' *Antiquities of the Jews* is the best source for checking that the New Testament is true. He mentions many significant characters, including details about John the Baptist.[5] Similarly, Tacitus mentions Pontius Pilate, the governor of Judea who allowed Jesus to be killed.[6] These writings confirm that many of the descriptions given to the key religious and political leaders mentioned in the New Testament are accurate.

Archaeological research has also supported many of the geographical details mentioned in the New Testament, which were previously questioned. For example, in the 1960s, an archaeological dig confirmed that there was a settlement in Nazareth (where the Gospels record that Jesus grew up) in the first century – previously, it was thought it didn't exist.

Sources outside the Gospels have largely helped to back up the detail found within the Gospels, indicating that they are reliable accounts.

How reliable are the copies of the Gospels we have today?

Even if the *original* Gospels were accurate portrayals of the events of Jesus' life, many people wonder whether the *copies* we have today are reliable, or whether they have been miscopied through the centuries. After all, every copy had to be written by hand, allowing plenty of room for human error.

Answers to two questions tell us how reliable ancient manuscripts are:

1. How many ancient copies of the document do we have?
2. What is the time span between the original document and the earliest surviving copy?

Taking this into account, let's compare the Gospels with other ancient historical works. Tacitus' *Histories* (written a few decades

later than most of the New Testament) has two ancient copies in existence, which were made about 700 years after the original. Caesar's *Gallic War* (written 100 years or so before the New Testament) has ten ancient copies in existence, the earliest of which was made about 900 years after the original. Both of these books are accepted by ancient historians as broadly accurate.

In contrast, there are 5,000 ancient portions of the New Testament in the original Greek language, and up to 20,000 portions in Latin and other languages. The earliest fragment of John's Gospel is dated to AD 130; and copies of the entire New Testament are dated to about AD 350, a mere 300 years after the originals were written.

If the surviving copies of Tacitus' *Histories* and Caesar's *Gallic War* are accepted as broadly reliable, then the surviving copies of the New Testament must be accepted as *incredibly* reliable. Importantly, all the various ancient copies of the Gospels in existence have a lot of agreement between them, showing that they are very reliable copies.

Why are there apparent discrepancies between the Gospels?

A careful reading of the four Gospel accounts side by side will reveal some differences. For example:

- not all of the Gospels record all the different trials that Jesus faced;
- only Matthew records the earthquake on the Sunday morning;
- the Gospels disagree over details such as the number of angels present at the tomb;
- none of the Gospels record all of the resurrection appearances.

Many people suppose that this means the Gospel records are unreliable.

The police wouldn't trust two witnesses who gave identical stories

In fact, quite the opposite is the case. Today, the police wouldn't trust two witnesses who gave identical stories about a suspicious event. Similarly, if all the Gospels were identical in what they reported, with no differences, we would conclude that they had deliberately 'fixed' their stories. Witnesses to any unusual event will have minor differences in what they report, because they will have seen things from different angles, and chatted with different people.

When we look at the four different Gospel accounts, we discover that they agree on the events, with only relatively minor differences over detail. Each Gospel writer has drawn on different eyewitness sources, and together they back up what the others say. Sir Edward Clarke, a former High Court judge, said:

> As a lawyer I accept unreservedly the Gospel evidence for the resurrection as the testimony of truthful men to facts they were able to substantiate.[7]

Verdict: is the evidence reliable?

I've given relatively brief answers to the most common questions about the reliability of the Gospel records, but I hope this is enough to help you draw your conclusions. Professional archaeologists, historians and language experts have studied the evidence in the Gospels for years, trying to establish how reliable they are. One scholar came to this conclusion:

> The evidence for our New Testament writings is ever so much greater than the evidence for many writings of classical authors, the authenticity of which no one dreams of questioning . . . If the New Testament were a collection of secular writings, their authenticity would generally be regarded as beyond all doubt.[8]

It should be clear by now that, as we read the pages of Matthew, Mark, Luke and John, we are reading very accurate and reliable accounts of the extraordinary events of the weekend in question. How then do we explain Jesus' empty tomb and resurrection appearances?

8. Dead . . . ?

If you've ever been a member of a jury, you'll be familiar with this sort of scenario: the defendant says that he didn't mean to kill the man; it was just self-defence. The prosecution says it was deliberate murder. Your role on the jury is to decide which of these two theories best fits the evidence.

When it comes to Jesus' alleged death and resurrection, we've heard the eyewitness evidence (Chapter 6), and know it's reliable (Chapter 7). I'd invite you now to take your seat on the jury as the cross-examination begins. Your task is to consider which of the competing theories about what happened to Jesus' body after his crucifixion is most likely to be true.

Theory 1: Jesus didn't actually die – he just fainted

The gist of this theory (sometimes called the 'swoon theory') has been around for at least 200 years. According to this theory,

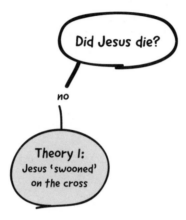

Jesus didn't die on the cross; he merely fainted in the heat. The cool of the tomb helped to revive him, so that his appearances three days later were not of someone who had come back to life from the dead, but simply of a man who had come close to death but fortunately survived.

The main problem with such swoon theories is that they have to pick and choose which parts of the earliest historical records to accept, and which to ignore. Consequently, no serious academics accept these theories.

It is also very hard to accept that Jesus did not die on the cross. His Roman executioners were experts in inflicting the death penalty. Evidence that supports Jesus' death includes:

○ As the Jewish authorities wanted the victims dead and buried before the Sabbath started, the executioners broke the victims' legs, leaving them unable to push themselves up to breathe. Death by suffocation would have followed quickly. However, when they came to break Jesus' legs, they saw that he was already dead.[1]

- To ensure he was dead, one of the soldiers pierced Jesus' side with a spear, drawing blood and water[2] – a medical sign that he had already died.[3]
- Jesus' death was unusually quick, causing Pilate to double-check with the centurion that Jesus had already died. The duty centurion confirmed Jesus' death.[4]
- The execution squad had an interest in ensuring that Jesus was dead: it is likely that they would have been killed had they let one of their victims escape with his life.

When these factors are weighed together, by far the most logical conclusion is that Jesus died.

However, if by some miracle Jesus had survived the crucifixion, the 'swoon' theory has further difficulties. For example:

- Jesus would clearly have needed expert medical help, yet none could have come from outside the tomb because of the sealed entrance and Roman guards.
- Jesus would need to have escaped from his grave clothes, which would probably have hardened around him into a mummy-like form.
- Jesus would need to have moved the heavy boulder from the entrance to the tomb – too much for one man to do.
- Jesus would need to have crept past the Roman guard, without being noticed.
- Having *escaped* death by the narrowest of margins, he would need to have convinced his followers that he had *triumphed* over death, showing no ill effects.

When we add all these things together we see that the 'swoon' theory is unlikely to be believable. Jesus really did die on the cross. This brings us to our second key question: was Jesus' tomb empty on the Sunday morning?

Theory 2: Jesus still lies dead in his tomb

Given that Jesus died, it is not unnatural to assume that his corpse remained, and still remains, in his tomb.

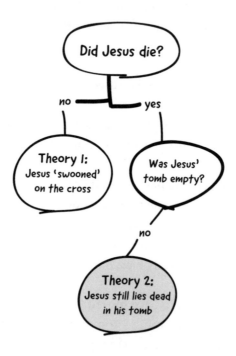

(a) The disciples accidentally looked in the wrong tomb

Some suggest that Jesus' followers were mistaken in thinking that his tomb was empty because they were looking in the wrong tomb. However, looking at the eyewitness evidence reveals that several different groups of people knew where the correct tomb was, and would have been able to identify it:

- Mark's biography states very clearly that Mary Magdalene was there when Jesus' body was laid in the tomb on the Friday evening, and that she was also one of the women who went to the tomb early on the Sunday morning.[5] To claim that her grief made her forget where her dear friend was buried within forty-eight hours is deeply patronizing!
- Joseph of Arimathea is even less likely to have forgotten the tomb in which Jesus was placed, because he owned it.[6]
- The Roman guards who were stationed at the tomb would not have left it once stationed there.[7]

To suppose that the tomb was not actually empty asks us to believe that *all* of these groups of people got the venue wrong, despite their interests in getting the right tomb.

If this theory was right, and Jesus was still lying dead and buried elsewhere, we would also have to find explanations for the disciples' strong conviction that they had seen Jesus risen again – which is easier said than done (see Theory 4). All in all, it is highly unlikely that Jesus' tomb still had his corpse lying in it.

(b) The disciples deliberately made up the story about Jesus' tomb being empty

Some people suggest that the disciples knew full well that Jesus' body was still in the tomb and just made up the story about its being empty. This questions the reliability of the Gospels' records, which contradicts the conclusions of the previous chapter. But there are other problems with this view as well, most of which will be expanded later in this chapter.

- Advocates of this theory would still need to find convincing explanations for over 500 people seeing Jesus alive after his death.

- The authorities would have gladly silenced the new movement by producing the body. That they *did* not is strong evidence that they *could* not.
- It is hard to imagine that the disciples could possibly have persuaded people that Jesus was alive again if they knew that he was still dead – yet they persuaded thousands.
- It is even harder to imagine that the disciples would have been willing to die a martyr's death for a cause they knew to be false – yet many of them did die for their convictions.
- The thousands of people who converted to Christianity after the disciples started preaching about the resurrection were all Jews who either lived locally, or were visiting. One scholar comments that these people

> were accepting a revolutionary teaching which could have been discredited by taking a few minutes' walk to a garden just outside the city walls. Far from discrediting it, they one and all enthusiastically spread it far and wide. Every one of those first converts was a proof of the empty tomb, for the simple reason that they could never have become disciples if that tomb had still contained the body of Jesus.[8]

For all these reasons, it is again best to conclude that Jesus' tomb was indeed empty by the Sunday morning. But how did it come to be empty? Our final key question is this: was Jesus' body removed?

Theory 3: Someone moved Jesus' body

Given that Jesus was really dead when he was placed in the tomb and that all the evidence points to his tomb being empty on the

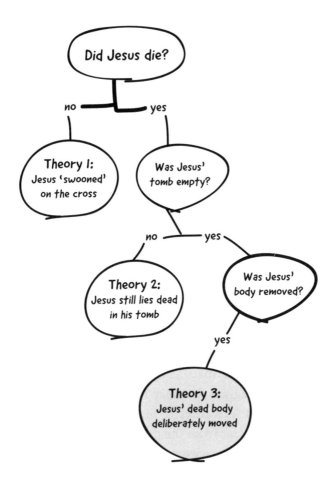

Sunday morning, many suggest that Jesus did not rise to life again, but that his body was removed.

A variety of different groups of people, each with their own motives, have been suggested as the possible culprits.

(a) Grave-robbers stole the body

Grave-robbing was not unknown in ancient times. With Pilate having posted the sign 'King of the Jews' over Jesus' head as he died, some might have been attracted by the (incorrect!)

thought that the king's grave would have contained riches worth stealing.

There are several difficulties with this theory:

- It is unlikely that robbers would have managed to pass the professional Roman guards.
- Why would the robbers have stolen a worthless corpse from the tomb, and left the valuable burial cloths behind?[9] They would have been daft thieves!
- Again, an explanation would still be needed for the disciples' meetings with Jesus, and the subsequent changes in their lives.

This theory has no evidence to support it, and plenty weighing against it.

(b) The disciples removed the body

Some people suppose that the disciples were expecting Jesus to rise again, so suggest that they removed the body to try to 'engineer' Jesus' resurrection for him.

However, it is clear from the disciples' reactions when they saw Jesus that they were *not* expecting him to come back to life. 'Engineering' his resurrection would have been the last thing to enter their minds.

Nevertheless, the idea that the disciples stole the body was the 'official' explanation given by the Temple authorities. Matthew's biography of Jesus records that the guards from the tomb

> went into the city and reported to the chief priests everything that had happened [i.e. the empty tomb]. When the chief priests had met with the elders and devised a plan, they gave the

DEAD . . . ? | 81

soldiers a large sum of money, telling them, 'You are to say, "His disciples came during the night and stole him away while we were asleep." If this report gets to the governor, we will satisfy him and keep you out of trouble.' So the soldiers took the money and did as they were instructed. And this story has been widely circulated among the Jews to this very day.[10]

As an explanation, it was pretty poor: the highly disciplined Roman guards faced severe discipline for sleeping on duty, and if they *had* all been asleep, how did they know *who* had taken the body?! And would they really have slept through several men shifting a massive boulder right next to them?

Other reasons to reject this theory include:

- The disciples had already shown themselves to be a cowardly lot in the face of soldiers, by running away when Jesus was arrested.[11] It is highly unlikely that they would have been brave enough to take on the guard after Jesus' crucifixion.
- If they did get past the guard, why were they never charged with theft of the body, which belonged to the authorities?
- If the disciples did remove the body, but proceeded to proclaim Jesus as risen, they would have been deliberately deceiving their hearers into believing a lie – something that does not fit well with the rest of their character.
- If a few of Jesus' friends did steal the body, a realistic explanation of the resurrection appearances to all the other people would still need to be found (see below).

Personally, I find this the least persuasive of all the theories that have been produced to explain the empty tomb.

(c) The authorities removed the body

Another theory is that the Jewish or Roman authorities moved the body. Perhaps the Jewish authorities wanted to move it so that Jesus' tomb couldn't become a shrine for his followers?

Within weeks of Jesus' death and claimed resurrection, thousands of people were switching from a traditional Jewish belief to a belief in Jesus as the Messiah. The Jewish authorities were powerless to stop the new movement, but could easily have done so simply by producing the body.

For the Roman authorities, the 'Jesus movement' obviously had political overtones, with people claiming that he was King of the Jews. They had as much desire as the Jewish authorities to clamp down on the new movement, because they feared it would lead to a popular uprising against their brutal occupation. So maybe they moved the body – again to even safer keeping?

But for much the same reasons as if the Jewish authorities had taken the body, it is also highly unlikely that the Roman ones did. As soon as the new movement began gathering pace (which it did very quickly), they could have produced Jesus' corpse and stopped the movement in its tracks. But they did not because they could not.

Theory 4: The disciples didn't really see Jesus alive

Those who say that Jesus remains in his tomb or that the body was stolen also have to explain Jesus' apparently healthy appearances. Many people have surmised that the disciples did not *actually* see Jesus alive again; they just *thought* they did – in other words, they were hallucinating.

But the historical accounts we have of Jesus' appearances do not merely involve people *seeing* him; they also include people *touching* him and *eating* with him.[12] Such physical contact would

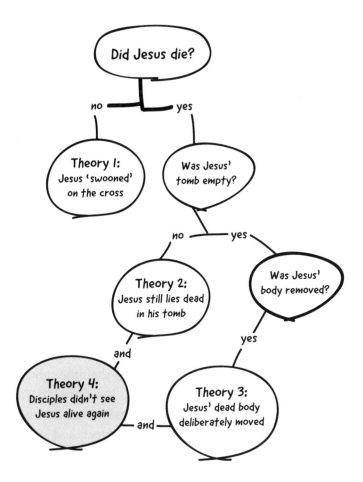

be impossible with an hallucination. Also, the appearances do not allow for accepted medical definitions of hallucinations because:

○ Hallucinations happen to individuals, not groups, yet the Gospel records tell us that Jesus tended to appear to groups rather than individuals. For example, he appeared to 500 people at once. It's impossible for 500 people to hallucinate the same thing at the same time.[13]

- ○ Hallucinations happen to certain types of individual – some are more susceptible than others. But the resurrection appearances were made to a wide variety of people – men and women; rugged fishermen, wily tax-collectors, seasoned debaters and others.
- ○ Hallucinations happen in certain circumstances, yet Jesus' appearances were very varied in their nature. That makes it extremely unlikely that the sightings could all be hallucinations.
- ○ Hallucinations tend to increase in severity over time, as the condition becomes worse, yet the historical accounts tell us that the sightings of Jesus stopped abruptly after forty days.

Of course, no-one expects to see a dead person alive again – not even Jesus' friends did. So on one of the first occasions when they saw the resurrected Jesus, it is not surprising that they assumed it was a ghost. But Jesus, knowing their thoughts, said to them, 'Look at my hands and my feet. It is I myself! Touch me and see; a ghost does not have flesh and bones, as you see I have.' Then he showed them his hands and feet, and ate some fish with them.[14] Jesus' friends soon became convinced that they were not just 'seeing things' – but that Jesus really had come back from the dead.

Together, these factors all point to the conclusion that the appearances to the disciples cannot simply be dismissed as hallucinations.

Conclusion

What happened after Jesus was sentenced to death? We've examined the competing theories but all of them have been

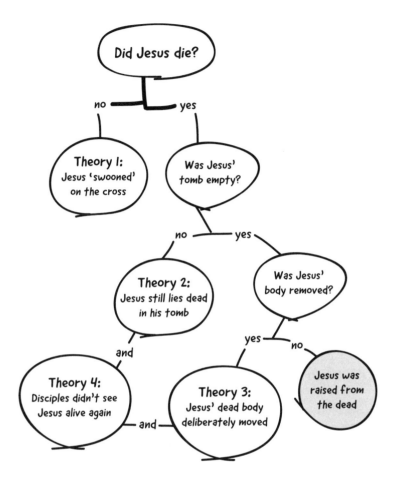

found wanting. We can be sure that Jesus did die on the cross on the Friday afternoon, yet that, by Sunday morning, his tomb was empty. It is extremely unlikely that grave-robbers or the disciples could have taken the body from under the watchful eyes of the Roman guards. If either the Roman or the Jewish authorities had removed the body, they would quickly have produced the body as proof to undermine the new movement's claims. In any case, the sightings of Jesus alive after his gruesome death also need an explanation – which cannot be mere hallucination on the part of hundreds of witnesses.

Could it be that the strangest explanation of all, the one that the disciples gave, is actually true? Was Jesus raised from the dead? It is now time to assess that claim in more detail.

Real lives – Albert

Albert Henry Ross wrote under the pseudonym Frank Morison.

'When I first began seriously to study the life of Christ, I did so with a very definite feeling that . . . his history rested upon very insecure foundations.' Albert was particularly dubious that the miracles really happened. He set out to write a book on the period of time immediately before and after Jesus' death, aiming to 'strip [the story] of its over-growth of primitive beliefs and dogmatic suppositions'.

However, when he came to investigate the events closely (a task he did so rigorously that many wrongly assumed he was a lawyer), he became convinced that the Gospel records were reliable, leading him to the surprising conclusion that 'there certainly is a deep and profoundly historical basis to [the statement] "The third day he rose again from the dead"'.[1]

He became especially dismissive of the idea that the key witnesses deliberately made the story up.

'No great moral structure like the early church, characterized as it was by lifelong persecution and personal suffering, could have reared its head on a statement every one of the eleven apostles knew to be a lie.'[2]

The book he eventually published became a classic. He tells his story in its preface:

'This study is . . . the inner story of a man who originally set out to write one kind of book and found himself compelled by the sheer force of circumstances to write quite another.

'It is not that the facts themselves altered, for they are recorded imperishably in the pages of human history. But the interpretation to be put upon the facts underwent a change. Somehow the perspective shifted – not suddenly, as in a flash of insight or inspiration, but slowly, almost imperceptibly, by the very stubbornness of the facts themselves.'[3]

9. . . . or alive?

I enjoy watching murder mysteries on TV. Any good story will rule out some obvious culprits, and turn up some surprising suspects. But even then, motives and method still have to be found; *could* thay have committed the crime?

When it comes to the mystery around Jesus' death and resurrection, we've ruled out some obvious theories (Chapter 8). In doing so, the bare facts of the case have been confirmed:

- Jesus died on the cross on the Friday afternoon;
- his corpse was put in a tomb shortly before sunset on the Friday;
- the same tomb was empty on the Sunday morning;
- his followers and friends believed that they saw him alive again after this;
- they were so convinced by what they had seen that they persuaded thousands of others that Jesus had risen from

the dead, and some of them were killed rather than give up their beliefs.

But *could* Jesus really have risen from the dead? It's time to look at some further objections, and call in some 'expert witnesses'.

'Surely miracles are impossible'

Our experience of this world is that dead people do not come back to life. Yet from a scientific perspective, it is actually bad science to say that 'dead people don't rise, therefore Jesus can't have risen'. Indeed, to believe that any miracle *can't* happen is as much an act of faith as to believe that they *can* happen.

Strictly speaking, no miracle (including Jesus' resurrection) is scientifically testable, because it claims to be a unique, unrepeatable event. Professor R. J. Berry of University College London and thirteen other leading Christian scientists wrote:

> Miracles are unprecedented events. Whatever the current fashions in philosophy or the revelations of opinion polls may suggest, it is important to affirm that science (based as it is upon the observation of precedents) can have nothing to say on the subject. Its 'laws' are only generalisations of our experience.[1]

So whilst science cannot *prove* Jesus' resurrection, it cannot *dis*prove it either.[2]

Sometimes it is suggested that people who lived in Jesus' day were less intellectually advanced than our generation, and therefore more likely to be taken in by apparent miracles. However, intelligent people ridiculed the idea of a resurrection on first hearing 2,000 years ago, just as many do today.[3]

But just because an event does not *normally* happen does not mean that it could *never* happen. There are many people who would claim to have seen events with no natural explanation.

Christians claim that God was intimately involved in the creation of the universe, and is still intimately involved in the continued life of the universe. He has set the laws of nature in place, but occasionally God chooses to work in ways for which we can find no 'natural' explanation. The Gospels record Jesus performing many such miracles – the blind seeing, the lame walking, even the dead reviving. Not even his opponents doubted that he performed these miracles or that they were supernatural. Could it not be that if Jesus is God, he could heal people instantly? Could it not be that if Jesus is God, the creator of life, he could give new life? As one of the first Christian leaders put it, 'Why should any of you consider it incredible that God raises the dead?'[4]

Certainly Professor Richard Swinburne of Oxford University, a philosopher, thinks it 'very probable indeed that Jesus Christ rose from the dead'.[5]

We're right to question the resurrection of Jesus carefully

Christians do not say that belief in the resurrection of Jesus is irrational or illogical. As it has never been repeated, it is not provable by science, and as it breaks the laws of nature, we are right to question it carefully.

But as a professor of law and humanities put it, 'The only way we can know whether an event *can* occur is to see whether in fact it *has* occurred. The problem of miracles, then, must be solved in the realm of historical investigation.' So, rather than asking scientists and philosophers whether the resurrection *could* have occurred, we would do better to ask historians and lawyers whether they think the resurrection *did* occur.

Listening to the experts: historians

Historians are trained and experienced in looking at accounts of past events, and assessing how reliable they are. Their role is to dismiss one version of events as highly unlikely and state that another account is far more likely to be true.

It is not surprising that many historians have examined the birth and growth of the Christian church, starting with examining Jesus. What do they make of the reports of his resurrection?

Drawing conclusions from eyewitness evidence
Professor Thomas Arnold of Oxford University was an expert in Roman history. He wrote:

> I have been used for many years to studying the histories of other times, and to examining and weighing the evidence of those who have written about them, and I know of no one fact in the history of mankind which is proved by better and fuller evidence of every sort, to the understanding of a fair inquirer, than the great sign which God has given us that Christ died and rose again from the dead.[6]

Verdicts like this help build our confidence in the likelihood of the resurrection having happened.

Drawing conclusions about the 'trigger' event
Historians also analyse the links between events, asking what caused something to happen. When analysing records of the

years that followed Jesus' death, historians note two unusual patterns:

- Within days of Jesus' death, all signs of grief were erased from his followers, and, within weeks, this tiny leaderless group had grown to thousands. It wasn't long before Stephen became the first Christian martyr, but not even that slowed the spread of the movement.[7]
- Although Jesus had mentioned that he would die and rise again, and although Jews had believed in the idea of 'resurrection' for centuries, it was not a major emphasis in Jesus' teaching or in the current religious climate. In other words, when the disciples preached that Jesus had risen bodily from the dead, this was a revolutionary teaching.[8]

The historian has to ask, 'What event could have triggered these unexpected patterns?'

Some people suggest that it was Jesus' *death*, not his *resurrection*, that was the event that pushed his disciples into action. However, historians say that Jesus' *death* alone wouldn't have been a sufficient trigger for the revolutionary message.

As Tom Wright (who has taught at the universities of Oxford and Cambridge, and is widely regarded as one of the leading authorities on the New Testament and events of those times) put it:

> As far as I am concerned, the historian may and must say that all the other explanations for why Christianity arose, and why it took the shape it did, are far less convincing *as historical explanations* than the one the early Christians themselves offer: that Jesus really did rise from the dead on Easter morning, leaving an empty tomb behind him.

He goes on:

> Of course, there are several reasons why people may not
> want, and often refuse, to believe this. But the historian
> must weigh, as well, the alternative accounts they themselves
> offer. And, to date, none of them have anything like the
> explanatory power of the simple, but utterly challenging,
> Christian one.

Elsewhere, he is even stronger in his conclusion:

> I have come to the conviction that the rise of the early church in
> the 40s and 50s is completely inexplicable, historically speaking,
> unless you have a strongly historical, bodily view of the
> resurrection of Jesus of Nazareth.[9]

Summary
Professional historians:

- affirm that the tomb was empty;
- state that alternative theories to explain the empty tomb
  are weak;
- affirm that people actually seeing Jesus alive again after
  his execution is the best explanation for the church's
  message and growth;
- conclude that Jesus rose from the dead.

But what of our second group of expert witnesses?

Listening to the experts: lawyers

What would lawyers conclude about the events of the first

Easter, trained as they are to discern truth from lies and reliable witnesses from false witnesses?

- A former Lord Chief Justice of England, Lord Darling, wrote about the resurrection:

  > We are not merely asked to have faith. In its favour as a living truth there exists such overwhelming evidence, positive and negative, factual and circumstantial, that no intelligent jury in the world can fail to bring in a verdict that the resurrection story is true.[10]

- Val Grieve, a lawyer, said:

  > I have carefully examined the evidence for the resurrection, the physical return from the dead of Jesus Christ . . . I claim that logic must point in the direction of his resurrection on an actual day and date in our history when, if you had been there, you could have touched the living Jesus and heard him speak.[11]

Again, these experts help boost our confidence in the likelihood of the resurrection accounts being accurate and true.

However, a full examination of the case in a court of law would not only draw on eyewitnesses, but might also call for 'circumstantial evidence'. In the case of Jesus' resurrection, this could include the following:

1. From Sabbath to Sunday
The Jewish holy day, reserved for worship, has for thousands of years been the Sabbath (dusk on Friday to dusk on Saturday). Yet the Christians started holding their main gatherings on a

Sunday. Why the change? It is because of the events of that first Easter Sunday. If there had been merely an empty tomb, the tone of Sunday worship would be puzzlement and unanswered questions. As it is, the tone is one of joy – at the fact of Jesus' resurrected life.

2. Jesus has remained significant for 2,000 years

The ancient world had plenty of religious movements and sects. But of all the new religions that were born around Jesus' time, only one has survived: Christianity. This shows the power of the Jesus movement. It has stood the test of time.

3. Christians today claim to know Jesus

It sounds strange, but the claim of millions of Christians today, from all around the world and from many different cultures, is that they know Jesus personally. The experiences of a small handful of them are included in this book. They each claim that Jesus speaks to them, listens to them, comforts them, directs them and challenges them. Above all, they claim that they are relating to a person who is alive and well, although they cannot see him. Intelligent adults who make these claims cannot be lightly dismissed. Christians will speak of their personal experience of Christ in a way that is compelling and cannot be denied. Would so many people claim such things if Jesus were still dead? We would have to conclude that they were all deluded and perhaps a little deranged.

Conclusion: a 'leap' of faith?

We have seen that all the evidence points towards the resurrection of Jesus really having happened. When it comes to assessing the claims of the disciples, historians and lawyers have given their firm support. As Sherlock Holmes said, 'When you have eliminated the impossible, whatever remains, however improbable, must be the truth.'

But where do we go from here?

Many people seem to think it is intellectual suicide to have faith, and imagine that to become a Christian involves a huge leap of faith.

In reality, however, all of us have faith. Whenever anyone walks across a bridge, they exercise faith in that bridge.

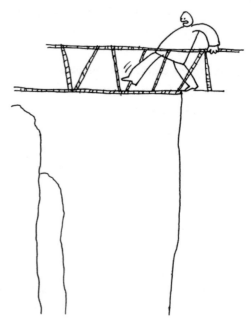

Imagine you are trekking in the mountains of Nepal when you come across a vast chasm with a flimsy-looking rope bridge strung between the two sides. The drop is hundreds of feet deep. Would you cross it?

As you stand there, some locals step onto the bridge and make their way across successfully. Having watched others cross the bridge, your faith grows. Taking a deep breath, you step out over the chasm. Your faith in the bridge is not suicidal, but reasonable.

When it comes to believing in the resurrection, we discover that the historical evidence and the experience of others who've put their trust in Jesus show that what was once imagined as a massive jump to faith turns out to be no further than a small step. Believing in the resurrection is not intellectually suicidal, but reasonable. The question facing you is whether you will rely on the evidence to take that step.

Thomas doubted, but when he saw Jesus for himself, he was convinced. Jesus then said to him something that reaches out to us: 'Because you have seen me, you have believed; blessed are those who have not seen and yet have believed.'[12] In other words, Jesus promises that those who believe in him and his resurrection today are blessed.

It is like those who venture onto the rope bridge in the Himalayas: the views are spectacular, but they can be seen only from the bridge. As a Christian, I can say that knowing Jesus is absolutely wonderful – but to get that knowledge for yourself, you'll have to take a small step of faith and join me on the bridge.

Are you willing to take the first step, by believing that Jesus rose from the dead? To change the metaphor, there can be no sitting on the fence on this issue: it either did or did not happen. In a court of law, a juror cannot abstain from voting. You have heard the evidence; what is your verdict: is Jesus dead or alive?

Real lives – Sir Lionel

Sir Lionel Luckhoo was a remarkable man. The hit cartoon The Simpsons *even ironically named one of its characters after him. The Simpsons', Lionel Hutz, never won a case; by contrast, the real-life Sir Lionel achieved 245 consecutive murder acquittals, prompting the* Guinness Book of Records *to hail him as the world's 'most successful' lawyer.*[1] *In addition, he was elected mayor four times, uniquely was appointed as High Commissioner for both Guyana and Barbados at the same time, and was twice knighted by the Queen.*

It was only at the age of sixty-four that Sir Lionel became a believing Christian, but 'the transformation was immediate. From that day my life changed – I moved from death to life, from darkness to light. I found real peace and happiness and joy'.[2]

For him, Jesus' empty tomb set Jesus apart from other religious leaders. 'Whereas the tomb of Muhammad in Medina holds the bones of Muhammad, and the tomb in Shantung holds the bones of Confucius and the tomb in Nepal holds the bones of Buddha . . . There are no bones in the tomb that once held Jesus, for he is risen.'

What did 'the world's most successful lawyer' make of Jesus' resurrection? He once wrote, 'I have spent more than forty-two years as a defence-trial lawyer appearing in many parts of the world and am still in active practice. I say unequivocally the evidence for the resurrection of Jesus Christ is so overwhelming that it compels acceptance by proof which leaves absolutely no room for doubt.'

But did he have any other evidence? Sir Lionel continued, 'I am often asked, how do you know Jesus lives? The answer I give is because Jesus is the risen Christ of the empty tomb, and . . . and this is most important, because he lives in my heart.'[3]

Part 3

So what?

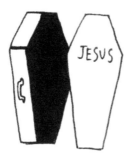

**What's Jesus' resurrection
got to do with me?**

10. What are the implications of Jesus' resurrection?

Over the last few years, we've been told repeatedly that the ice caps are melting. At first, that hardly seemed relevant to us; after all, not many of us are polar explorers who are suddenly going to be unemployed. But slowly, we're realizing the implications of the ice caps melting: sea levels rising, and millions of people's homes being flooded.

I want to show you that the fact that Jesus rose from the dead has serious implications for us too. To explore this we're going to join a devoutly religious man called Saul travelling along Damascus Road with some friends a couple of years after Jesus' death. As he was travelling, he saw a blinding flash of light – and it wasn't a speed camera . . .

Many years later, Saul (by then called Paul) was telling his story.[1] He admitted that he *had been* what might now be called a religious fundamentalist. But his fundamentalism was misplaced: he had used violence to impose his Jewish views on other people, particularly Christians. As he put it, 'I . . . was convinced that I ought to do all that was possible to oppose the name of Jesus of Nazareth . . . On the authority of the [religious leaders] I put many of the [Christians] in prison, and when they were put to death, I cast my vote against them.'

Not the nicest of people. And certainly not a believer in Jesus.

'On one of those journeys,' Paul continued, 'I was going to Damascus . . . About noon . . . as I was on the road, I saw a light from heaven, brighter than the sun, blazing around me and my companions. We all fell to the ground.' Paul 'heard a voice' saying to him, 'Saul, Saul, why do you persecute me?'

Unable to see and baffled as to who was speaking, Paul asked, 'Who are you, Lord?'

Then came the moment that must have felt like an earthquake in Paul's mind. The voice replied, 'I am Jesus.'

Imagine it: the same man that Paul had opposed so intensely was now speaking to him! Paul couldn't deny his experience – apart from anything else, he was temporarily blinded. Paul had thought Jesus was dead and buried, but he was forced to change his mind: Jesus was in fact well and truly alive. Three days later, Paul became a Christian, and was to become one of the most influential Christians in history.

Implications about Jesus

Paul also became a prolific letter-writer, leaving us a clear record of some of the important new conclusions he came to about Jesus.

1. Who Jesus is

In Chapter 1 I said that Jesus' resurrection was the final proof of his outrageous claim to be God in human flesh. Some of the very earliest documents describing Jesus as God are those written by Paul himself. In one letter, he described Jesus as 'the image of the invisible God'.[2] When Paul met the risen Jesus he was forced to realize that Jesus wasn't the evil man he once thought. Rather, he was, and is, God himself.

What's your view of Jesus at the moment? Is it changing as you read this book?

2. Jesus is alive today

At the risk of stating the obvious, another of the implications of Jesus' resurrection is that he's still alive today. His victory over death was permanent. After forty days of people meeting the risen Jesus on earth, he was taken up to heaven before his friends' eyes,[3] but they were absolutely clear that he hadn't died a second time.

Paul's own dramatic experience convinced him that Jesus is alive. For example, he talks of speaking to Jesus and hearing him speak, of living to please Jesus, and of Jesus' continued activity through his church.

Christians today say the same things. They do not follow a dead man; they worship the risen Jesus, who is very much alive.

Christians do not follow a dead man

How does it make you feel to think of Jesus as alive, and watching over our lives?

3. Jesus will come back one day

To Paul, Jesus' resurrection and continued life in heaven were closely connected with a strong belief that Jesus would come back again. Jesus clearly thought that human history as we know it would have an end, marked by his return.

He spoke about his return in vivid language:

But in those days . . .

    'the sun will be darkened,
        and the moon will not give its light;
    the stars will fall from the sky,
        and the heavenly bodies will be shaken.'

At that time people will see [Jesus] coming in clouds with great power and glory.[4]

Many people scoff at the idea that Jesus will one day come back to this earth. But Jesus predicted many things in the course of his life that did come true. In fact, his own second coming is the only prophecy he made that has yet to be fulfilled. So Paul wrote, 'We eagerly await a Saviour from [heaven], the Lord Jesus Christ.'[5]

But what will happen when Jesus returns?

- *We will face Jesus as our Judge.* Reading the Gospels, it's very striking that Jesus takes it for granted that he will be our judge when we face him on his return.[6] He reassures us that his judgment will be fair, 'for I seek not to please myself but him who sent me'.[7]
- *A separation will take place.* Jesus makes this clear: 'When [Jesus] comes . . . [all] the nations will be gathered before him, and he will separate the people one from another as a shepherd separates the sheep from the goats. He will put the sheep on his right and the goats on his left.'[8] Paul also believed that a separation would take place,[9] with two possible destinies: an unimaginably glorious heaven[10] and a horrendously awful hell.[11]

So how will Jesus make his judgment? He said that his judgment and separation will be based on our response to him and his teaching: 'If anyone is ashamed of me and my words in this . . . generation, [I] will be ashamed of him when [I come].'[12] In other words, Jesus' verdict on us then will be directly related to our verdict on him now: if we're ashamed of him now, not wanting to know him, then he'll be ashamed of us then, not wanting to know us.

Such a judgment makes sense to us. If a friend snubs you publicly one day, they couldn't really expect you to help them out of a tight spot the next – at least, not without at first apologizing. Similarly, we shouldn't expect Jesus to accept us if we've spent most of our life ignoring him!

Paul realized that Jesus' resurrection didn't just have *theoretical* implications about Jesus; it had *personal* implications for him as well. Jesus' resurrection affected Paul's eternal destiny. The same is true for us. If Jesus rose from the dead, Christianity is shown to be something infinitely more important than a simple 'take it or leave it' lifestyle choice. If Jesus rose from the dead, he's God over us, alive and reigning in heaven, one day to return and judge us on the basis of our response to him. That statement should be enough to make us all sit up and take notice!

But, as Paul discovered, Jesus' resurrection has more implications.

Implications about us

When I was a teenager, I remember my parents sitting down with me and telling me that Dad was leaving his job. But as the discussion went on, it became clear that we might have to move. All of a sudden, the knock-on effects became all too apparent: I might have to move away from my friends. I was devastated.

When Paul met the risen Jesus, I suspect he was equally devastated when he began to figure out the knock-on effects of what he now knew to be true about Jesus himself.

1. The way to know God is through Jesus

When Paul understood that God had supremely revealed himself in Jesus, he suddenly realized that the way to know God now was through Jesus. He wrote,

> There is only one God,
> and Christ Jesus
>   is the only one
> who can bring us
>   to God.[13]

Indeed, Jesus had said that the *only* way to know God was through him: 'I am the way and the truth and the life. No-one comes to the Father except through me.'[14]

The implication for us, then, is that if we want to know God, we can do so *only* through Jesus.

2. By nature, we are separated from God

Most of us think that we're pretty decent people. In our minds, we take that a step further: we suppose that because *we* think fairly highly of ourselves, so does *God*. Those of us with any religious background presume that counts in our favour as well.

Paul thought in exactly that way before his life-changing experience. He claimed, 'I did everything the Law demands in order to please God.'

But Jesus' resurrection changed his entire mindset. He carried on, 'But Christ has shown me that what I once thought was valuable is worthless . . . I could not make myself acceptable to God by obeying the Law.'[15] Paul realized that pleasing God now entailed pleasing Jesus – which was exactly the opposite of attacking Jesus' followers! It's not surprising that years later he described himself as 'the worst of sinners'.[16]

'Sin' is a word often used by Christians, but what exactly does it mean? Jesus says that people are sinful 'because people do not believe in me'.[17] So sin isn't breaking one of God's moral *rules* by pretending they don't exist. Sin is breaking God's *heart* by ignoring him. If we really believed in Jesus, we'd understand that his moral rules are put there for our *benefit* (in much the same way as a mother tells her child not to play near the cooker), and we'd then seek to live by them. When we don't seek to live by them, it's a sure sign that we don't really believe in Jesus.

Someone once said that 'the heart of the human problem is the problem of the human heart'. Jesus would agree, because when our hearts don't truly believe in him, the consequence is that we ignore the pattern for living that he's given us. The result is that our sin separates us from God, and the punishment for sin is death.[18] That sounds harsh at first, but just as committing treason against one's nation by betraying your homeland deserves to result in punishment from the state authorities, so committing treason against God by rejecting his rightful authority over our lives deservedly results in divine punishment. Paul knew that unless apology was made and pardon granted, all sin would be punished: we would remain separated from God even beyond death.[19]

3. We are spiritually dead

Paul used to think that he was well connected to God and pleased him. But the revelation that he'd actually been hurting God made him realize that all along he'd been spiritually dead, not spiritually alive. As he put it years later when writing to Christians, 'In the past you were dead because you sinned and fought against God.'[20]

Once again, Paul's new conclusion reflects what Jesus himself had taught. Speaking to someone who considered himself very spiritual, Jesus told him that 'no one can see the kingdom of God without being born again'. Jesus went on to make it clear that he wasn't suggesting that people be *physically* born again – that would be impossible. What was necessary was that everyone was 'born of the Spirit'[21] – in other words, that they have a spiritual birth.

Jesus was clear, and Paul now agreed with him: if someone hasn't been spiritually born, they're not yet spiritually alive, and therefore as good as dead!

How does that verdict make you feel?

An 'earthquake' experience

When telling the story of Paul's encounter with Jesus, I described the moment of his realization that Jesus was alive as being like an earthquake in Paul's mind. Earthquakes have obvious instant effects as well as more subtle long-term effects.

Paul's life-changing meeting with the risen Jesus had a series of instant effects:

- He realized that Jesus wasn't an evil man but God in human flesh;
- He realized that Jesus wasn't dead in his grave, but alive and reigning in heaven;
- He realized his judgment of Jesus had been completely wrong and inappropriate. One day Jesus would return to earth, and judge him on his response to Jesus.

But the whole lie of the land in Paul's mind changed as well:

- He realized that the way to know God was through Jesus, not through obeying rules;
- He realized that his previous attempts at pleasing God were useless, and that, far from being near perfect, he was in fact the worst of sinners;
- He realized that he was spiritually dead.

These implications of Jesus' resurrection are incredibly profound and far-reaching – not just for Paul, but for each one of us. That Jesus was raised from the dead turns out to have an effect on our eternal destiny! But it also tells us a lot about our life now and how we can get to know God.

Of course, it feels awful to be declared 'spiritually dead'. But Paul's experience should in fact give us great optimism. After all, when he encountered the risen Jesus, he experienced a love so deep that he was forgiven and his life was turned around. As he put it,

I used to say terrible and insulting things about him, and I was cruel. But he had mercy on me because I didn't know what I was doing, and I had not yet put my faith in him . . . Jesus . . . was very kind to me. He has greatly blessed my life with faith and love just like his own.[22]

He stopped attacking Christians and started encouraging people to become Christians; he quit trying to close churches and began to found them instead.

Paul's 'earthquake' experience was doubtless very painful for him. But it turned out to be for his good. He couldn't be 'born again' until he'd acknowledged he was spiritually dead. But, having realized his terrible mistake, he received Jesus' gift of new life. He was no longer dead but alive: 'We were dead because of our sins, but God loved us so much that he made us alive with Christ.'[23]

But how exactly can Jesus make us alive? To answer that question, we need to wind the clock back thirty-six hours from Easter Sunday morning to Good Friday afternoon.

Real lives – Miguel

Miguel worked for seventeen years as a fishing/marine engineer in Brazil. Nine years ago he helped start a new church; it now has over 1,000 members.

Miguel, what do you make of Jesus?

As a young adult, I never went to church, and considered religion unnecessary for being a good citizen. I played basketball, and spent much time travelling the Brazilian coastline looking for waves and anything connected with the surf culture.

Entering university, I decided to study marine/fish engineering. At university I met up again with many friends, and some of them seemed to have something different about them: they spoke of Christ, and their lives had changed. It had quite an impact and attracted me greatly, especially the fact that they seemed to really 'live'.

I began going to a Christian group and became interested in Jesus' words, so I began to read the Bible. I read the whole of the New Testament and I was mesmerized by the stories, and by Jesus Christ. I was amazed by his power over everything from disease to the weather. And whoever he met – those suffering injustice, the hopeless, the sick, the lost, children – he always had a face of love.

One day, I was invited to a prayer gathering for young people, and there, in the middle of a prayer, I felt the presence of Jesus Christ more alive than anything, and I was scared to open my eyes for fear of seeing Christ himself in that room. A young man spoke some prophetic words which addressed me directly, speaking about my life and my anxieties.

I handed my life over to Jesus there and then, and asked him to give me the strength to live my life for him. Something happened inside me, a certain conviction that Jesus was alive and with me in that place, a conviction that continues today, every waking moment of my life.

Jesus, alive and present, has been the absolute certainty of my life.

11. Life from death

For years, it was assumed that Harold Shipman's elderly patients were dying of 'natural causes'. In reality, the truth was far more sinister. After an inquiry, deaths were reclassified as murders.

What was Jesus' cause of death? In Chapter 10, we saw how Paul changed his views about Jesus and himself, having encountered the risen Jesus. In this chapter, we'll see how Paul also had to reclassify Jesus' death. He came to realize that it wasn't a straightforward death penalty. The truth was far more wonderful.

So why did Jesus die?

The wrong answer

Before Paul's conversion, he would have approved of Jesus' death with a look of smug satisfaction. People from the same religious sect as Paul had worked hard to ensure that Jesus was crucified. Paul's approval of Jesus' death was on the grounds that Jesus had been a 'blasphemer' – someone who claimed to be God when in fact he wasn't. To Paul's intensely religious mind, that was the worst crime imaginable – and worthy of immediate death.[1] However, when Paul came to realize that Jesus was alive again, his opinion of Jesus' death as God's deserved judgment was shattered.

The film *In the Name of the Father* recounted the story of 'The Guildford Four' – four men who were wrongly convicted of being involved in an IRA bombing. After fifteen years in prison, the verdicts were overturned and they were released. Their release was proof that they'd now been declared innocent of the crime.

Similarly, when Jesus was released from the grave, it was the most stunning overturning of a sentence imaginable – and showed beyond doubt that God declared him to be innocent of the crime for which he was killed.

In fact, the historical accounts of Jesus' trial leave no doubt that Jesus was innocent.[2] Pilate, known as a ruthless ruler, found 'no basis for [the] charges' against Jesus, and gave in to the stubborn request for the death penalty only because he was swayed by peer pressure.

Elsewhere, the Bible underlines that Jesus was innocent of *all* wrongdoing. Before Jesus began his public ministry, he faced a series of temptations, none of which he gave in to. Jesus himself stressed that he was obedient to his heavenly Father. One Christian writer said that Jesus 'has been tempted in every way, just as we are – yet was without sin', describing him as 'holy, blameless, pure, set apart from sinners'.[3]

So Paul came to realize that Jesus didn't die because he was guilty. Rather, his resurrection indicated the exact opposite: that Jesus was completely innocent. The one perfectly innocent man who ever lived took the ultimate punishment.

Paul was left with a mystery that has puzzled many people since: Why did Jesus *have* to die?

An inadequate answer

One common answer to that question through the years has been that Jesus died as an example of sacrificial love, in order to encourage us to be more loving towards one another. But that answer by itself is inadequate. An illustration will help explain why.

Suppose I take my wife for a romantic weekend in Paris, and we climb the Eiffel Tower. Then suppose that I turn to my wife and say, 'I want to show you how much I love you', and with that I jump off the tower, and plunge to my death.

It wouldn't be a sign of love, would it? It would be a sign of madness! A death by itself doesn't demonstrate love.

But of course, a death *can* demonstrate immense love if the person dies whilst protecting or rescuing someone else. Imagine instead that my wife and I go for a moonlit stroll along the River Seine. If, whilst gazing adoringly into my eyes, she accidentally fell in, and if I manfully rescued her but drowned in the process – well, that *would* be demonstrating love, because I would have saved her. She would have benefited from my death.

Paul certainly agreed that Jesus' death was a sign of love[4], but realized that, for it to be loving, someone else must benefit from his death. Jesus had sacrificed himself, but for whom?

A more complete answer

The startling answer that Paul came to was that Jesus 'Christ died *for us*'[5] and again that 'he died *for all*'.[6] Paul came to realize that Jesus had sacrificed himself for everyone, including you and me.

While he was alive, Jesus himself had taught about his own death. He described himself as the 'good shepherd' and said he was going to 'lay down [his] life *for the sheep*'.[7] When Jesus died,

it was a demonstration of his immense love *for us*. Paul's touching personal confession of faith can be echoed by any Christian: '. . . the Son of God . . . loved *me* and gave himself for *me*'.[8]
But how exactly do we benefit from his death?

The full answer

At the back of Paul's mind was the burning problem that he was a 'sinner' – out of sorts with God – and he knew that his sin must be punished. But there was a delightful puzzle as well: when Jesus appeared to Paul, we might have expected him to strike him down, considering what he'd done to Jesus' followers. Instead, Jesus had apparently accepted Paul into his service!

When Paul added all this together, the conclusion he came to and subsequently preached to thousands was that Christ died '*for our sins*'.[9] What was happening as Jesus died was a great exchange: Jesus was receiving the punishment for our offences against God. As Paul put it, 'Christ never sinned! But God treated him as a sinner.'[10] Paul understood our rejection of God to be incredibly serious and forgivable only at a cost. In the past, that cost had been the life of many innocent animals. But now Jesus himself was giving his life 'to be a sacrifice for our sin'.[11]

So Jesus took our guilt and punishment from us. But what was the other part of this exchange? Amazingly, it's that we're treated as Jesus should have been: we're declared innocent and put right with God, free from all punishment. Our guilty past is wiped out, enabling our friendship with God to be resumed. As Paul wrote, 'God was reconciling the world to himself in Christ, not counting people's sins against them.'[12]

Once more, Paul's conclusion wasn't original, and was almost certainly founded on the teaching of Jesus. When Jesus shared his last meal with his closest followers, shortly before he was arrested and convicted, he'd explained what was going to happen. In a deeply symbolic gesture, he'd taken bread and wine, and likened them to his own body and blood. He said his body was going to be broken, and his blood 'poured out for many for the forgiveness of sins'.[13] Hours later, this picture became real on the cross.

What Jesus was achieving as he died was an exchange of the most enormous proportions. Here, then, is the heart of the Christian faith. As Jesus died, he took on himself the punishment for Paul's offences – so that Paul's friendship with God, both before and after death, could be restored. We can only imagine the flood of emotions Paul felt as he first truly understood why Jesus had died. Later on, he could barely contain himself, writing, 'Thanks be to God for his indescribable gift!'[14]

But Paul also knew that the way his own life had been turned around by Jesus' death and resurrection was proof that anyone's life – maybe even yours – could be similarly changed. As he put it, 'Since I was worse than anyone else, God had mercy on me . . . so that others would put their faith in Christ and have eternal life.'[15]

Our sin makes us spiritually dead, but Jesus died for all, to blot out our past offences and give us the possibility of renewed spiritual life – life in friendship with God. Do you long for your past offences to be wiped out, and guilt taken away? Deep down, do you wish you could find unconditional and constant acceptance and friendship? Paul found those when he realized why Jesus had died. Paul was made spiritually alive.

Jesus' death: the moment of new life

When I was growing up, our family visited Yellowstone National Park. As it happens, forest fires were raging. To me, the fires

were rather exciting; to the average tourist, the fires were a tragedy. Thousands of trees and hundreds of animals were killed. However, those who knew the park well were less disappointed. Forest fires are a natural part of the life of such ecosystems. The pine trees in the forest release their seeds only under considerable heat, such as in a fire. So as the old trees were being burnt, they were releasing the seeds of new life. Today, the landscape isn't full of old, dead trees, but of a vast number of healthy young trees – trees that could be planted only because of the fire.

We've been exploring the question of why Jesus died. As with those forest fires, his death was not the tragedy that it seemed. It was, in fact, the *only* way new life could start. As he died, Jesus made it possible for us to be 'born again', to become spiritually alive – reconnected with God.

Jesus himself knew that his death would be the peak of his life's work and the moment of new birth. His warning that his future would be full of suffering was particularly insistent.[16] For him, this future wasn't optional. He *had to* suffer and *had to* be killed.

Jesus held on to that conviction even as he hung on the cross. As he died, Jesus shouted out, 'It is finished.'[17] In Jesus' day, that phrase was used much as we use the phrase 'Paid in full' to declare a debt cleared. In other words, it's a shout of triumph, not failure. He knew that, as he died, he was paying in full for the sins of the world. His resurrection proved that his sacrifice had been acceptable to God.

One of the most moving bits of poetry in the entire Bible provides us with a wonderfully clear explanation of what Jesus' death achieved:

But the fact is, it was *our* pains he carried –
   our disfigurements, all the things wrong with us.
We thought he brought it on himself,
   that God was punishing him for his own failures.
But it was our sins that did that to him,
   that ripped and tore and crushed him – *our* sins!
He took the punishment, and that made us whole.
   Through his bruises we get healed.
We're all like sheep who've wandered off and gotten lost.
   We've all done our own thing, gone our own way.
And God has piled all our sins, everything we've done wrong,
   on him, on him.[18]

It's no wonder that Christians from the first days to now have wanted to tell everyone the good news: anyone who trusted that Jesus had taken the punishment for their sins when he died would have their sins forgiven and be guaranteed eternal life. 'Everyone who believes in him receives forgiveness of sins through his name,' they said. 'Believe in the Lord Jesus, and you will be saved.'[19] They told others this news, because they knew it was true for themselves.

Faith in Jesus' death: the means of new life

One final point must be made as we close this chapter. Although God's offer of forgiveness is available to everyone, it's *not* given to us automatically. A few years ago, my building society was floated on the stock exchange. All their existing customers could apply for shares which wouldn't cost anything to buy, but could be sold on at 100% profit. It was as close as you could get to 'free money' – but you had to apply. Similarly, God offers us a free gift – but we have to 'apply' for it.

God offers us a free gift – but we have to 'apply' for it

The 'application process' is simple: all one has to do is 'believe in the Lord Jesus'. As Paul put it, 'God accepted me simply because of my faith [= belief] in Christ.'[20]

Such a message is wonderfully liberating, for if we had to work to be forgiven by God, we'd never think we'd done enough to earn it. The cross gives us absolute confidence that God now accepts us.

The most famous verse in the Bible underlines this point. Speaking in advance about the results of his own death, Jesus said, 'For God so loved the world that he gave his one and only Son, that whoever believes in him shall not perish but have eternal life.'[21] Later, he said, 'Very truly I tell you, whoever hears my word and believes him who sent me has eternal life and will not be judged but has crossed over from death to life.'[22] However, there's a flipside to that promise: 'Whoever does not believe stands condemned already because they have not believed in the name of God's one and only Son.'[23]

In this chapter, we've discovered how Paul was, and how we can be, made 'alive with Christ': through trusting in the fact of Jesus' sacrificial death. We can contribute nothing, for Jesus has already paid in full: 'We were dead because of our sins, but God loved us so much that he made us alive with Christ.'[24] So Jesus was raised from the dead. Paul was made alive in Christ. But what about *you*?

As we've unpacked the implications of Jesus' resurrection, it's become clear that the real question is no longer 'Is *Jesus* dead or alive?' It's now this: 'Are *you* dead or alive?'

Real lives - Terry

Terry is a lifeguard in Liverpool and in his spare time tells schoolchildren and youth groups about Jesus' power to change lives. His story has been reported in many countries.

Terry, why is Jesus' death so important to you?

I was an accidental pregnancy and my dad was violent towards me. I hung out with local gangs and was arrested at twelve for car theft and thirteen for drug use. I was expelled from school, sacked from my first job, and got involved with football hooliganism. After the 1985 Heysel Stadium tragedy in which thirty-nine Italian football fans died, I was the first person charged with manslaughter, and was given a jail sentence. When I was released, I became a drug dealer. Having been raided by the police, I went on the run to Europe.

Hoping there was a better way to live, I returned to

Liverpool and handed myself in. Before I was sentenced, I met some Christians who said they'd pray for me! Amazingly, my drugs case was dismissed, so I went to a local church. It wasn't what I expected – but I felt a peace and acceptance. The preacher spoke about how, because of Jesus' death, God forgives us, changes us and gives us the hope of heaven. Jesus seemed to be the answer for my life. I became a Christian.

The people in church were loving and patient. My life slowly changed: eventually God broke every addiction, and physically and psychologically I recovered. God's helped me be more caring and is making me less selfish. He even restored my family relationships, and my father accepted Jesus as his Saviour three days before he died. Twenty years on from Heysel, I went to Italy to apologize for what I'd done.

The death of Jesus reveals to me how much God loves me. Jesus' death in my place means a way has been made for me to become a child of God. 'Amazing love! How can it be that you, my God, should die for me?'

12. Dead or alive?

Jesus was an amazing storyteller. In this chapter, I'd like us to listen to one of the most famous stories he ever told.[1] 'There was a man who had two sons,' he began. The father in the story represents God, and the two sons denote two typical responses to God. Let's think about which of the two sons we are most like and whether – in relation to God – we're dead or alive.

'Dad, I wish you were dead'

> The younger son said to his father, 'Father, give me my share of the estate.' So he divided his property between them.

For a son to go to his dad in the Middle East 2,000 years ago and ask for his share of the estate was like saying he wished his dad was dead. The younger son would have brought shame on the entire family by asking for his inheritance early.

The younger son represents those who push God out of their lives, so that they can live life how they want.

It can be a fun position to be in. The younger son wasn't in the slightest bit concerned about his dad; his only concern was having a good time.

> Not long after that, the younger son got together all he had, set off for a distant country and there squandered his wealth in wild living.

Many people are in exactly that place today – living for themselves, caring nothing for God.

Are you in that position? In your desire to get the most out of life, have you deeply offended God by ignoring him?

'What am I playing at?'

Or maybe for you the party finished long ago.

> After he had spent everything, there was a severe famine in that whole country, and he began to be in need. So he went and hired himself out to a citizen of that country, who sent him to his fields to feed pigs. He longed to fill his stomach with the pods that the pigs were eating, but no-one gave him anything.

At some point in life, we all learn that the party can't go on for ever. The younger son learnt that lesson. He was deeply unhappy, starving and desperately lonely. We can tell how low he'd fallen – the thought of eating pig food is disgusting enough for us; for him as a Jew, it was forbidden.

It often takes some external event in our life to make us come to our senses. The younger son experienced physical disaster and financial ruin. Others face personal failure, tragic loss, or a crippling illness. But the results are often the same: unhappiness, emptiness and loneliness. Can you identify with those?

The one good thing about being at rock bottom is that you can only go in one direction – up. The question is: how?

> When he came to his senses, he said, 'How many of my father's hired men have food to spare, and here I am starving to death! I will set out and go back to my father and say to him: Father, I have sinned against heaven and against you. I am no longer worthy to be called your son; make me like one of your hired men.' So he got up and went to his father.

Here's the key: ' . . . he came to his senses'. Rather than ignoring his problems, he thought about where he had gone wrong, and what he could do to put it right. He knew that he'd be much better off back home.

That's the way it is between us and God: many people think that being a Christian would be a living nightmare, full of petty rules and with little freedom. But the reality is that living away from God always results in inner turmoil. We'd all be better off 'back home' with God – living as he made us to live, in relation-ship with him.

So the younger son swallowed his pride and decided to go home. He knew that he deserved to be turned away. The only thing he could take with him were words of humble apology.

If you've rejected God, what sort of reaction would you expect if you turned back to him? Blazing anger? Fierce judg-ment? A blocked entrance?

'I want you back, son'

The younger son found none of these responses, and Jesus wants us to understand that, if we turn back to God, we too receive a warm welcome:

> But while he was still a long way off, his father saw him and was filled with compassion for him; he ran to his son, threw his arms around him and kissed him.

To me, this is one of the most moving verses in the Bible, because it pictures a God who loves me so much that:

- he's been looking out for my return ever since I walked out on him;
- he doesn't care what other people think of me (everyone else would have been scandalized by the son's behaviour);
- he's willing to humiliate himself (for a grown man to run at that time was shameful) – just as Jesus was humiliated on the cross;
- he doesn't mind what state I'm in (the younger son would have stunk after his disgusting work and long walk home);
- he embraces me personally.

That's how much he loves you, too. Could this be the answer to our deep inner longings?

This overwhelming welcome had even occurred before the son could give his apology:

> The son said to him, 'Father, I have sinned against heaven and against you. I am no longer worthy to be called your son.'

But the father cut him off mid-sentence. It was up to the father to set the terms of welcome:

> But the father said to his servants, 'Quick! Bring the best robe and put it on him. Put a ring on his finger and sandals on his feet. Bring the fattened calf and kill it. Let's have a feast and celebrate.'

Earlier on, the son had enjoyed wild parties in distant countries, but here was the real party, one that welcomed him home not as a hired worker but as an honoured son.

And the punchline?

For this son of mine was *dead* and is *alive* again; he was lost and is found.' So they began to celebrate.

This is the incredible welcome that awaits us if we return to God, and the amazing reversal in our status when we do so. We may be spiritually dead now, but God makes us alive again.

But maybe you don't recognize yourself in the mirror so far. You're not partying; nor are you hurting. You're just working.

Out in the cold

Meanwhile, the older son was in the field. When he came near the house, he heard music and dancing. So he called one of the servants and asked him what was going on. 'Your brother has come,' he replied, 'and your father has killed the fattened calf because he has him back safe and sound.'

The older brother became angry and refused to go in. So his father went out and pleaded with him. But he answered his father, 'Look! All these years I've been slaving for you and never disobeyed your orders. Yet you never gave me even a young goat so I could celebrate with my friends. But when this son of yours who has squandered your property with prostitutes comes home, you kill the fattened calf for him!'

It's easy to feel a bit sorry for the older son, who clearly felt hard-done-by. But all the time he'd been working for his dad, he'd been missing the point. He clearly didn't love his father, so he saw his work as 'slaving'. He wasn't able to *receive* his father's love because he was trying so hard to *achieve* it.

It's an easy mistake to make. If you didn't recognize yourself in the mirror as the younger son, maybe you recognize yourself now.

'My son,' the father said, 'you are always with me, and everything I have is yours. But we had to celebrate and be glad, because this brother of yours was dead and is alive again; he was lost and is found.'

If that's you, Jesus reassures you of God's love, but then cuts the story short without telling us what happened to the older son. That was deliberate: if you identify with the older son, Jesus leaves *you* to finish the story. Will you *receive* God's love and join the party, or stay out in the cold, trying unsuccessfully to *earn* God's love?

Will you receive God's love and join the party?

Looking in the mirror

Jesus told this story to get us thinking about where we stand with God. So, as you look in the mirror, whom do you see? Whether you see the younger son having the time of his life or sitting unhappily by the pigsty, or whether you see the older son outside in the cold, something needs to be done. You need to come home.

Real lives – Deborah

Deborah is a family doctor whose interests include reading, entertaining and avoiding lawn mowing.

Deborah, how did you become a Christian?

I attended church from an early age. One occurrence really helped to crystallize my faith. My Sunday-school teacher was recounting a memorable event from her own childhood. She'd been unwell and was sleeping in her parents' bed that night. She became anxious regarding what would happen to her if Jesus were to come again. She tried to reassure herself that, should this happen, she would hold on to her mother's night-dress and be taken along with her. Soon after having this thought she heard a voice saying to her, 'It's no good; you'll have to go alone.' At that point she made her own personal commitment to being a follower of Christ.

Listening to her story, I understood clearly for the first time that God was interested in a relationship with me *firsthand* . . . there could be no hiding behind my mother's skirts or 'hand-me-down' Christianity. It was what I believed personally that was important. I knew at that point that I wanted to have my own special relationship with God. I began having my own personal 'talks' with God, telling him about my worries and saying sorry for the things I'd done wrong. I knew absolutely that he was always with me.

Over the years my understanding of God and how we are saved through his Son, Jesus, has grown. At university, it would have been easy to drift away, but I always came back to what I knew was true – Jesus died for me so that I could be free from sin and know God intimately. There have been many ups and downs since but I have never forgotten the lesson that I was taught that Sunday at church. That God should desire such a personal relationship with me is a source of constant wonder.

13. Meeting the risen Jesus

Possibly the hardest jigsaw puzzle I've ever done was a double-sided jigsaw: you first had to work out which picture a piece belonged to, then put the pieces in place.

In the last few chapters, we've looked at different jigsaw pieces of the Christian faith, but sometimes it's hard to see that they all belong to the same picture. Let me summarize where we've got to by putting the pieces in order, so we can see and understand the big picture.

- *Jesus' life* shows us what God is like. He's full of indiscriminate compassion, reaching out to people of every age, race, background, sex and lifestyle.
- *Jesus' teaching* comes as a rude awakening. As well as great advice on how to live, he gives the verdict that we are all spiritually dead because we've rejected the God who made us.

- *Jesus' death* was the climax of his mission. He died an innocent man, taking the punishment of the guilty. Jesus' death offers us forgiveness for sins, freedom from guilt, healing of past hurts and the conquering of death. By faith in his death, we can be made alive and put back in touch with God.
- *Jesus' resurrection* is the best explanation for what happened to him after his dead body was put in the tomb. It is also the only explanation for the radical change that happened in his followers. Jesus' resurrection tells us that Jesus is alive and watching over us now. After his resurrection, he was taken up to heaven, from where he now rules the earth.
- *Jesus will come again* to bring this world as we know it to its fulfilment. Jesus will judge all people everywhere fairly, based on our prior response to him. Those who've rejected him will in turn be rejected *by* him and experience the grim reality of hell; those who've accepted him and followed him as their Lord will enjoy the paradise of heaven.
- *God longs for us to know him* with a deep and active passion. Jesus' story in the last chapter didn't just show us our own heart; it gave us a glimpse of God's heart as well. He loves us deeply; he longs for us to return to him; he's filled with overwhelming joy and forgiveness when we do so.

When you see those jigsaw pieces fitting together, and take a step backwards to look at the whole, what picture do you see? At its centre stands the risen Jesus, with his arm outstretched towards you, and his nail-scarred hand beckoning you towards him as he calls you by name.

It's the most incredible picture, and we instinctively know that it demands some sort of response.

Responding to God

When a man asks a woman to marry him, there are in the end only two answers – 'yes' or 'no'. The woman will think carefully about her response (we hope!), because it's such a major decision. Responding to Jesus is a bit like that. He asks each one of us to make a momentous decision – whether or not to follow him. As with getting married, the implications are huge and lifelong. So what's involved in following him? Jesus used two phrases that sum it up: 'Repent and believe the good news' and 'Follow me.'[1] Let's unpack what he meant.

1. 'Repent' – sorrow for the past

To 'repent' means to change direction – to do a 'U-turn'. So when Jesus tells us to 'repent', he's telling us to change our *minds* about him, and change the direction of our *lives* to follow him. That's exactly what the younger son did in Jesus' story.

Repenting takes great humility. But the only way there can be reconciliation between us and God is if we say sorry, acknowledging both the hurt we've caused him and how much it cost Jesus to win forgiveness for us.

2. 'Believe the good news' – looking to the cross

The next step is to believe the good news about Jesus Christ – that he is God in human flesh, who was born into our world,

lived a perfect life, suffered death in order to grant us forgiveness, rose to new life and will come again as our judge.

In the Bible, 'belief' involves the mind, the heart and the
body. A genuine Christian puts their belief about Jesus into
action: they say that he's God, and then prove their belief by
putting Jesus' teaching into practice day by day.

3. 'Follow me' – change in the future

The younger son in Jesus' story understood the implications of
returning to his father. In looking to be accepted back into his
home as a hired worker (or, indeed, as a son), he would be
coming under his father's authority and agreeing to live by his
rules again. When Paul summarized what he told people to do
in response to God, he said, 'I preached that they should repent
and turn to God *and prove their repentance by their deeds.*'[2]

Jesus said, 'Whoever wants to be my disciple must deny themselves and take up their cross and follow me.'[3]

'Denying self' means saying 'no' to our own desires, ambitions
and priorities, and asking instead, 'What would Jesus want?' It's
putting Jesus' interests above our own. To follow Jesus is to
make him number one in our life, rather than ourselves – and
that applies to every area of life

In time, Jesus will examine our heart, looking at the way we
conduct our relationships. At some point, he'll have a look at
our mind – the way we think. He'll want to examine our mouths
(what we say), our eyes (what we look at and read), our
ears (what we listen to). He'll want to enter our pockets, to help
us change how we use our money. He'll look at our hands and
feet, to see how we use our bodies physically. Slowly, he'll look
at every part of our lives, and prompt us about changes we need
to make if we're serious about following him.

'Denying self' is hard work, but Jesus is realistic about the task.

○ He doesn't expect every change to happen *instantly* and certainly doesn't wait for us to be perfect before accepting us. Change is a lifelong process.

○ He doesn't expect us to be able to change *alone*, but helps us. New Year's resolutions tend to fail because we attempt to keep them in our own strength. Christians have God's help to change – the same helping power that raised Christ from the dead![4]

Because we have God's help, the changes involved in following Jesus aren't impossible. The 'Real Lives' stories in this book show that God really does turn ordinary people's lives around, helping us to break powerful addictions, overcome crippling fears and find a healthy self-image.

Paul's experience was that becoming a Christian was the best decision he ever made:

> Christ has shown me that what I once thought was valuable is worthless. Nothing is as wonderful as knowing Christ Jesus my Lord. I have given up everything else and count it all as rubbish. All I want is Christ and to know that I belong to him.[5]

I decided to follow him years ago, and have never regretted it for a moment either. But what will *your* decision be?

Making a decision

It's right to make a carefully considered response, for it's a decision that will shape the rest of your life. But, as you consider whether to become a Christian, remember also the implications of *not* doing so.

Some reading this book might genuinely need more time to think about the costs involved – but please don't delay the decision for too long. You will find it useful to go to an Alpha course or Christianity Explored course or some other Christian basics course in a local church to help you come to your decision.[6] Jesus offers us a wonderful gift and lifelong friendship, but, just as the man who's proposed to a woman may allow her some time to think carefully, he eventually requires a straight 'yes' or 'no' answer.

Jesus offers a wonderful gift and lifelong friendship

Some people think that they can put off their moment of believing until just before they die. Yet although God will readily accept 'deathbed conversions', not many of us know when we'll die, and whether we'll have time to 'repent and believe' at that point. In any case, how can anyone delay receiving the most precious gift we can ever receive, having genuinely understood how much it cost Jesus to buy? It would be the height of insolence! Those who want to delay committing themselves to Jesus have not fully understood the dangerous place they're in. The very name 'Jesus' means 'the Lord saves' or 'the Lord rescues'[7] – and a drowning man wants to be rescued as soon as possible, not to put it off as long as possible.

Far from delaying our decision, the Bible urges us to get right with God as soon as possible:

Seek the LORD while he may be found;
call on him while he is near.[8]

If you're ready to become a Christian, do so!

Meeting the risen Jesus

The way to tell Jesus that you want to become a Christian is by speaking to him. It doesn't matter whether you speak out loud, or quietly in your mind – he's God, so he'll be able to hear you. You might want to base your prayer on this one (it summarizes what we've said in this chapter), adding in your own personal confessions in the blanks:

> Jesus,
> I now recognize that you are God,
> yet that I have rebelled against you.
> I'm sorry for the wrong ways I've treated you [. . .]
> I'm sorry for the wrong ways I've treated other people [. . .]
> Thank you so much for loving me and dying for me on the cross.
> I believe that, through your death,
> my relationship with you can start over again.
> Please help me to stop going my own way
> and start following you.

If you've made that prayer your own, the chances are you don't feel any different, but that's not to say your prayer hasn't 'worked'. Our feelings go up and down but our faith rests on God's promises, which are firm and solid. Let me finish with a reminder of some of God's promises:

- 'Whoever comes to me I will never drive away.'[9] This reassures us that Jesus welcomes everyone who comes to him.
- 'For God so loved the world that he gave his one and only Son, that whoever believes in him shall not perish but have eternal life.'[10] This reminds us of God's deep love for us.

- 'If we confess our sins to God, he can always be trusted to forgive us and take our sins away.'[11] This assures us that God has pardoned us and completely forgotten about our previous rejection of him.
- 'I am the resurrection and the life. Anyone who believes in me will live, even though they die; and whoever lives by believing in me will never die.'[12] Based on Jesus' own victory over death, this reassures us of life beyond the grave.

Is *Jesus* dead or alive? The evidence of his empty tomb and the changed lives of his followers both then and now declare that he's alive.

Are *you* dead or alive? Jesus said, 'Very truly I tell you, whoever hears my word and believes him who sent me has eternal life and will not be judged but has crossed over from death to life.'[13]

Congratulations!

Postscript: What next?

If you've become a Christian, welcome to the family! I've made it clear that it's a decision that will affect the rest of your life – for the better. But what should you do over the next few days?

After the first ever Christian sermon, 'those who accepted [the] message were baptised . . . They devoted themselves to the apostles' teaching and to the fellowship, to the breaking of bread and to prayer'.[1] Let me say a few words on these four aspects, and give you some Bible passages to look at.

1. Go public

As a new Christian, you must make some sort of public declaration of your new faith – it's a way of nailing your colours to the mast. To start with, tell a friend (maybe a Christian you know?) what you've done. Often, telling someone else makes your decision seem more real to you as well. In due course, when you've settled in a local church, you may need to be baptized as a further public declaration of your new faith.

'Going public' with your faith is an ongoing part of the Christian life. Once we have received such a precious gift ourselves, and know that it's freely available to all, it would be selfish of us not to tell others! But 'gentleness' and 'respect' are to be our hallmarks when speaking to others about Jesus.

Some Bible passages to read on going public: Matthew 28:18–20; 1 Peter 3:15–16.

2. Listen to God

The new Christians then 'devoted themselves to the apostles' teaching' – teaching that we now find in the Bible. As we read and study the Bible, we hear God speaking to us. We must listen to him for guidance about how our life needs to be reformed, and what direction our life should take. Make time each day to read the Bible, asking that God would help you understand it and live it.

Start by reading one or two of the Gospels, then the rest of the New Testament, in a modern translation of the Bible. Getting some 'Bible-reading notes' will help you understand and apply what you're reading.[2]

Some Bible passages to read on the Bible: 2 Timothy 3:14–16; Psalm 119:97–106.

3. Join in the family activities

As a new Christian, you should join a local church, because belonging to a church is a key part of keeping going and growing as a Christian. A good church will teach the Bible carefully.

A good way to get to know people in your new church, and to go over the basics of the Christian faith again, is to join a group for new Christians or those considering the Christian faith. When you visit a church, introduce yourself to the minister, and explain that you've recently become a Christian.

Some Bible passages to read on belonging to a church: Romans 12:3–13; Acts 2:42–47.

4. Talk to God

Prayer is talking to God from your heart. Like any father, God longs to hear from his children. However, just as a loving parent doesn't always give their child what they ask for, nor will God, because not everything we ask for is actually *good* for us. In time, it will become more obvious what sort of things you should ask for in prayer.

An obvious time to pray by yourself is before and after you've read the Bible each day – but you can carry on praying short prayers through the day whilst on the bus or doing the washing up! It can be very encouraging to pray with others as well.

Some Bible passages to read on prayer: Luke 11:1–13; 18:1–14.

Notes

Introduction
1 Acts 17:18, emphasis added.
2 John 10:10.
3 1 Corinthians 15:14 (CEV).

Chapter 1: Is there anybody out there?
1 Mark 1:22.
2 Mark 5:42.
3 Mark 4:41.
4 Mark 3:22.
5 Mark 2:7 (CEV).
6 Matthew 28:9.
7 John 20:24–28.
8 Romans 1:4; Colossians 1:15–19; Philippians 2:6.
9 e.g. Matthew 9:36; 14:14; 15:32; 20:34; Mark 1:41; Luke 19:41; John 11:33–38.
10 e.g. Mark 15:40–41; Luke 8:2–3; 10:38–42; John 11:5.

Chapter 2: Why hasn't God done something about all the suffering?
1 Psalm 44:23–24 (CEV).
2 Isaiah 53:3.
3 Hebrews 2:17–18 (The Message).
4 2 Corinthians 1:3–4.
5 Hebrews 2:14.
6 Acts 2:24.
7 Hebrews 2:9.

8 1 Corinthians 15:54–55, 57.
9 Revelation 21:1, 3–5.

Chapter 3: What happens when we die?
1 1 Corinthians 15:22.
2 Matthew 13:49–50.
3 Matthew 13:44.
4 1 Corinthians 2:9 (CEV).
5 Revelation 7:9 (CEV).
6 Revelation 21:4 (CEV).
7 Revelation 21:3–4 (CEV).
8 Mark 8:34–38.
9 John 11:25–26 (TNIV).

Chapter 4: Does life have a meaning or purpose?
1 Interviewed in the Sunday Times News Review, 21 October 2004.
2 Prince Charles, quoted by Rico Tice.
3 Bernard Levin, quoted in Nicky Gumbel, Questions of Life, (Kingsway, 2001), pp. 13–14.
4 Interviewed in The Times, 15 September 1998.
5 John 10:10.
6 Luke 12:15 (TNIV).
7 Luke 12:33.
8 Matthew 6:33.

9 Interview shortly before his death, quoted in Gumbel, *Questions of Life*, p. 15.
10 2 Chronicles 20:7.
11 John 17:3, emphasis added.
12 Matthew 6:9.
13 Philippians 3:8 (CEV), emphasis added.
14 Exodus 34:6–7.
15 Selwyn Hughes, *Light on Life's Ultimate Questions* (CWR, 2002), p. 27.
16 Augustine, *Confessions*, I:1 (1).
17 John 6:35 (TNIV).

Chapter 5: Which religion, if any, is true?

1 Chapter 7 will assess the reliability of these accounts in much more detail.
2 Romans 1:4.
3 Michael Green, *The Empty Cross of Jesus* (Hodder, 1984), pp. 129–130.

Chapter 6: Looking at the evidence

1 Flavius Josephus, *Antiquities of the Jews* xviii:63.
2 Cornelius Tacitus, *Annals of Imperial Rome* xv:44.
3 Josephus, *Antiquities of the Jews* xviii:63.
4 Phlegon, a second-century Greek historian, whose writing is known by its quotation in Origen's *Against Celsus*, suggests that Jesus prophesied; that the darkness and earthquakes around the time of Jesus' death and resurrection did happen in Tiberius' reign; and that Jesus

was crucified and rose again. The Jewish Talmud says that Jesus was executed on Passover Eve. Pliny, in the early second century, described Christians as worshipping Christ as God.
5 Throughout this section, I will draw heavily from the Gospel accounts: Matthew 26 – 28; Mark 14 – 16; Luke 22 – 24; John 18 – 21.
6 This section and the next also draw on 1 Corinthians 15:5–8.

Chapter 7: Is the evidence reliable?

1 Some scholars suggest much earlier dates even than this.
2 Craig Blomberg in Lee Strobel, *The Case for Christ* (Zondervan, 1998), pp. 42–44.
3 Luke 1:1–2 provides evidence for this.
4 Luke 1:1–4.
5 Josephus, *Antiquities* xviii:117ff.
6 Tacitus, *Annals* xv:44.
7 Sir Edward Clarke KC, quoted in John Stott, *Basic Christianity* (IVP, 1971).
8 F. F. Bruce, *The New Testament Documents*, (IVP, 1981), p. 10.

Chapter 8: Dead . . . ?

1 John 19:31–33.
2 John 19:34.
3 See Lee Strobel, *The Case for Christ* (Zondervan, 1998), pp. 198–199 for a medical explanation of this.
4 Mark 15:44–45.
5 Mark 15:47 – 16:1.
6 Matthew 27:57–60.

7 Matthew 27:62–66.
8 G. R. Beasley-Murray, *Christ is Alive* (Lutterworth Press, 1947), p. 63.
9 John 20:5–7.
10 Matthew 28:11–15.
11 Matthew 26:56.
12 e.g. Luke 24:30; John 20:27; 21:13.
13 See Strobel, *The Case for Christ*, pp. 238–240.
14 Luke 24:36–43.

Real Lives – Albert
1 Frank Morison, *Who Moved the Stone?* (Authentic Lifestyle, 1996), p. 192.
2 Morison, *Who Moved the Stone?*, p. 89.
3 Morison, *Who Moved the Stone?*, preface and Chapter 1.

Chapter 9: . . . or alive?
1 R. J. Berry in a letter to *The Times*, 13 July 1984.
2 Famous scientists with a Christian faith have included Galileo Galilei, Sir Isaac Newton, Michael Faraday, and many others alive today.
3 Acts 17:32.
4 Acts 26:8.
5 Richard Swinburne, *The Resurrection of God Incarnate* (OUP, 2003), p. 214.
6 Thomas Arnold, *Sermons on the Christian Life* (Fellowes, 1842), p. 342, quoted in McDowell, *The Resurrection Factor* (Paternoster, 1993), p. 21.
7 The story of the beginnings of the church is told in Acts 2 – 8.

8 The early preaching of the Christian message in Acts is notable for its emphasis on eyewitness reports of Jesus' resurrection.
9 N. T. Wright, *New Heavens and New Earth* (Grove, 1999), p. 4.
10 Lord Darling, quoted in Michael Green, *The Day Death Died* (IVP, 1982), p. 15.
11 Val Grieve, *Your Verdict* (STL / IVP, 1988), p. 17.
12 John 20:29.

Real Lives – Sir Lionel
1 *The Guinness Book of Records 1990*, p. 211.
2 Lionel Luckhoo, *What is Your Verdict?* (Fellowship Press, 1984), p. 19, quoted in Ross Clifford, *Leading Lawyers' Case for the Resurrection* (CILTPP, 1996), p. 112.
3 Lionel Luckhoo, *The Question Answered* (see www. hawaiichristiansonline.com).

Chapter 10: What are the implications of Jesus' resurrection?
1 This narrative is taken from Acts 26:4–15.
2 Colossians 1:15.
3 Acts 1:9.
4 Mark 13:24–26 (TNIV).
5 Philippians 3:20.
6 e.g. Matthew 7:21–23.
7 John 5:30.
8 Matthew 25:31–33.
9 e.g. Romans 2:5–11.
10 e.g. Romans 8:18–21; 1 Corinthians 2:9.

11 e.g. 2 Thessalonians 1:8–9.
12 Mark 8:38.
13 1 Timothy 2:5 (CEV).
14 John 14:6.
15 Philippians 3:6–7, 9 (CEV).
16 1 Timothy 1:16.
17 John 16:9 (TNIV).
18 Romans 6:23.
19 2 Thessalonians 1:8–9.
20 Ephesians 2:1 (CEV).
21 John 3:3, 8 (TNIV).
22 1 Timothy 1:13–14 (CEV).
23 Ephesians 2:4–5 (CEV).

Chapter 11: Life from death

1 It's clear in the Gospels that there were previous plans and attempts to take Jesus' life before the one that was successful (e.g. Mark 3:6; John 8:59; 10:31). They all arose from Jesus' allegedly blasphemous claims.
2 See, for example, Mark 14:55 – 15:11 and Luke 23:4–47.
3 Hebrews 4:15; 7:26.
4 e.g. Ephesians 5:2.
5 Romans 5:8; 1 Thessalonians 5:10; Titus 2:14.
6 2 Corinthians 5:15, emphasis added.
7 John 10:14–15, emphasis added.
8 Galatians 2:20, emphasis added.
9 Romans 4:25; 1 Corinthians 15:3; Galatians 1:4, emphasis added.
10 2 Corinthians 5:21 (CEV).
11 Romans 8:3 (CEV).
12 2 Corinthians 5:19 (TNIV).
13 Matthew 26:28.

14 2 Corinthians 9:15.
15 1 Timothy 1:15–16 (CEV).
16 e.g. Luke 9:22; 17:25; 22:15.
17 John 19:30.
18 Isaiah 53:4–6 (*The Message*), emphasis added.
19 Acts 10:43; 16:31.
20 Philippians 3:9 (CEV).
21 John 3:16.
22 John 5:24 (TNIV).
23 John 3:18 (TNIV).
24 Ephesians 2:4–5 (CEV).

Chapter 12: Dead or alive?

1 Luke 15:11–32.

Chapter 13: Meeting the risen Jesus

1 e.g. Mark 1:15–17.
2 Acts 26:20, emphasis added.
3 Mark 8:34 (TNIV).
4 Romans 8:11; Ephesians 1:18–20.
5 Philippians 3:7–9 (CEV).
6 See www.alpha.org or www.christianityexplored.com.
7 Isaiah 55:6.
8 Matthew 1:21.
9 John 6:37.
10 John 3:16.
11 1 John 1:9 (CEV).
12 John 11:25–26 (TNIV).
13 John 5:24 (TNIV).

Postscript: What next?

1 Acts 2:41–42.
2 See www.thegoodbook.co.uk or browse in a local Christian bookshop for some examples of Bible-reading notes.